They

★

Jesus Today

★

two essay

★

Traumear

*

We may arrive at the conclusion eventually that we wish to come out from among those who judge according to appearances and make a world that is composed of those who are ruled by others and those who rule others. Such a resurrectional development takes time and we do well to gain some understanding of what to expect from those who participate in this world and are part of it in every way.

In addition, as we evolve to our full human maturity, we may realize that we have much of this world within us and we would like to be rid of it. The very spirit that stimulates our resurrection is on one hand willing to cleanse us and on the other hand eager to help us understand what we are up against as we come into our inheritance. This essay takes us right to the point of arrival, where we now have what it takes to turn and create a modus vivendi for ourselves alongside 'Them'.

*

Index

They   pg. 1

Jesus Today   pg. 41

*

They

This book sets out to describe the relationship that exists at present between those who are ruled by others and those who rule others. It proposes to include in this description not only the every-day state of things, observed in a detached manner, but also certain achieved possibilities of personal involvement, arising out of the study of the matter at hand and ending always in communicably expressed conclusions. No hypothesis is ever assumed and no theory is attempted. The effect of the book resides exclusively in the reading process.

The great majority of Them on the earth today are consciously influenced by someone else with regard to their outward behaviour. How They respond to this influence, be it negatively or positively, be it intelligently, automatically, or in disinterested reaction, it is the case every time that someone else is to a degree held responsible. To be totally responsible oneself for this influence is a burden not long to be endured. And those who are in this way influenced do also in some way influence the outward behaviour of others. Here too someone else is to a degree held responsible. Those who rule and those who are ruled are in fact the very same. They differ only with respect to the context of their activity. Therefore we do well not to disturb the essential integrity of those we may describe as 'regular'.

Out of context, all regular behaviour gradually becomes inaccessible to our awareness. It must remain fixed as a means towards an end if we are wisely to comprehend it. Consequently it neither upsets nor discourages us if the discrepancy between what we find and what we would like to find is from time to time very wide indeed.

*

Let us begin by discussing what is meant in our day by the word public. How do we react to the concept, when an unguarded moment brings us face to face with it? One man shrinks because he has something to hide. Another experiences the expansion of his soul because he has something to offer. A third adjusts the attitude of his personality and is pleased that his conscience is clean. Yet another prides himself on the past achievements of his character, and gratefully he embraces his ego. One even speaks of the public as such, treating it as an entity in its own right, endowed with judgment – above all with judgment, with feelings which can be hurt or flattered, with a mind of its own, fickle and dangerous though readily assuaged by guile. At any rate the public must be pleased, or else it strikes back. Approach it cynically, and it gains you respect. Face it hypocritically, and the public praises you, for you show no wrong; it backs you up because you do not act as if you were letting it down.

And yet who is there among us who is not himself a member of the public? Of course, it is argued, the public is the sum-total of individual humanity, and our jobs, professions, careers and titles are only recognizable to us because of this public, which we honour so that it may honour us. Society today rests entirely on the successful separation of the private realm from the public. Society is envisioned as perfect when awareness, consciousness, and even knowledge of this separation is finally uprooted, eradicated and wiped out. The social contract is a mutual agreement on effacement and evasion. There is no bond left between those we mean that contributes in any way to the achievement of happiness or to the attainment of strength.

Then on what basis do They communicate? How does it come that They know of each other, and indeed how do They know of each other? Is it not true that we must share some common ground, be it ever so elusive, before we can even meet, not to speak of exchanging something of value for mutual benefit? So you say that we all are human beings. Surely this is enough reason for the initiation of love, and every child knows that love conquers all. Is it true that They all appear to be human beings? Of course They do, one only needs to look at them. Never mind that most of them stare back in disbelief. We look human, They seem to say, and we hope that this will fool you.

There are some who speak of a duty to society. But consider the nonsense They promulgate. There may be a duty to one's fellow man, to one's neighbour if you please, and that in itself is society; so how can there be a duty to society? All these are high-sounding lies to keep an idol alive. To what degree have these idols claimed the available effectiveness of their mind? How often have they in fact succeeded in replacing the mind? Ask one of Them who allegedly is a member of society to reveal to you his principles and priorities. Primarily he wishes to survive. So does the worm in the soil. Except that the worm cannot really be credited with the capacity of a wish – and in truth can we seriously wish to survive? No, it is an inclination of the flesh prior to the birth of intelligence. How many of them understand the difference between living and surviving, when living, to them, means survival in security, pleasure, comfort and contentment up to and excluding death? Today They identify with their bodies – or else They will have no part of the body, and quite regularly both are the case. Priority number one is health. Good health to them is a prerequisite for good living, rather than its consequence. Principle number one is material self-sufficiency. They desire to live in such a fashion that everyone else is dispensable. Is this not the desire to own the world which ends with the grave? The power for isolation lures the soul away from its task and transforms it into the shell for the vacuum, so that nothing may enter or leave. In this vacuum They feel justified. Secretly They hope that judgment cannot reach them. In fact even now They are judged.

So whether you work for your survival or else survive for your work, it amounts to the same, which is a doctrine of absolute nihilism. Sentiments of kindness, a belief in the ultimate progress of the human race, an insistence upon my right to prefer what I like, to like what I prefer; these must save me. Let the pessimist rant, Let the optimist prate. In the pinch I can always fall back on my animal instincts, When faced by the impossible, the hypothetical supremacy of the intellect will surely see me through. There is hope even in revenge beyond the grave, and courage may be drawn from the deserved pre-destination of my own flesh and blood, may it not? As I was born, oh Lord, so I return to you, a little stained by circumstantial abuse, mind you, and how could I help it, Lord, you are merciful, but basically I am innocent in my own eyes.

The one outstanding ailment affecting their relationships today is distrust. An exceedingly curious phenomenon occurs, in that this ailment not only attacks and corrodes, but actually has become in itself the hallmark of their character and the institution of their personality. The carrier of the ailment is unmitigated fear. It is the fear which cannot be recognized or dealt with because it disrupts the senses and paralyses the will. In other words, They are afraid without knowing it and while They are afraid They can do nothing except fear. Hence They cannot even admit to anyone that They fear, hence sympathy and encouragement are out of the question. The memory however is marked by every event, instance and occasion of this fear, and hence the approach of distrust. The code of politeness suggests that They respect each other's memory of this unknowable fear. What They mean by friendship dictates that the memory of this

4

fear is not only respected, but actually related. They join in what They call friendship insofar as They have been afraid on similar terms. The marriage contract strictly and coldly enforces that two of them become one in the memory of this fear. Every unwillingness to act or behave as if this fear had never existed must be ruthlessly exploited by the marriage partner and marriage is said to work when two of them of the opposite sex are able to completely fool and befuddle each other as to the nature of their intentions and the meaning of their deeds.

They need politics. Without politics They soon lose their sense of self-esteem, and those without self-esteem are worthless to each other. Political leadership in their case is really a contradiction in terms, since leadership implies somewhere to go, while politics must insist upon reference to the status quo. Food and shelter are the politically essential aims, while more food and shelter are the signs of political progress. The law is not feared anymore, but its counterpart, the collective hatred, malice, resentment and spite, has taken its place in their hearts, on account of their desire to upraise themselves at the expense of another, be it as individuals or as political states. The law cannot combat its own disintegration. No government can enforce a law which is morally questionable. So where their political interests are concerned, morality plays second fiddle. This is where the relative gist of politics comes quite clearly out into the open. It is the only field of activity where absolute egotism and humanitarian appeal may blithely go hand in hand. The argument of general utility will always hold its own against particular selfishness. Hence the barrier of misfit rationality between those who must rule and those who must be ruled. Imagination is required to understand this. Participation in life as a fragmentary thing, which is what all of their political activity and concern amounts to, cannot be reasonably deduced from any concept of life as a whole. A great deal of literary perspiration has been wasted in attempts to do just this. Politics is like a love affair, narcissistic in origin, in retrospect both bitter and dreamy, and Echo keeps calling from afar. It is the story of the mule and the carrot, but there is no one to benefit from the telling of it. Those who must rule are whipped by the scourge of responsibility, while those who must be ruled are beaten by the flail of their rights. The ideology of the moment takes its toll in terms of minds lost and bodies wasted so that no one may accidentally become boss of the world or grand wizard of the earth's council chamber. How difficult it must be for Them not to act as if They were preparing for one of these two positions: They tell us what *you* can do and what *you* cannot do, what *you* can say and what *you* cannot say, all because of this and that, and never do They say that *I* can do this or that. They themselves must undeniably stay out of the picture.

Whoever must rule does so from the sidelines. Whoever wishes to rule does so because he cannot mind his own business. We wish it were otherwise. Only regard the influence of nation upon nation, of state upon state. Look behind the mask of the peace-seeking world community. One is easily beguiled because today one does not often find there the simple savagery and unadulterated selfishness which a healthy wisdom and smartness have in the past taught us to expect. Neither is it a case of animal idolatry or of sovereign greed. In the absence of these classic vices one might be forgiven for entertaining anticipations of a pleasant surprise. However gradually one comes to realize that it is the mask alone that is left. And it is not any more presented as a mask by those who wear it, but They themselves believe to our astonishment that They show us their real faces. Any attempt to shake them in this belief seems at first of debatable value. Upon reconsideration we are convinced that such an

6

attempt would indeed be tantamount to foolishness. If a man refrains from insulting me openly because he fears public censure, I must still guard against his intention and inclination in private but if he does not insult me because he mistakes his pretence of kindness for real kindness, then I have nothing further to worry about; at least as far as the insult is concerned. There remains, of course, the strange infectiousness of this half-breed lie. A response of real kindness simply is washed away and goes under while the gullible innocent stands perplexed. Duplicity would have pained him, and he might have learned to understand this pain and to forgive its origin, but in this case there is no immediate pain which might be associated with duplicity; instead the very ability of kindness which was practiced is paralyzed and rendered effete. A silly sort of euphoria sets in, a bland religiosity or a virtuosity at empty socializing develops, and the end-product is charisma, mystique or stardom. Given all three in one, this would readily answer to their expectation of the returned Christ.

Let us only for a moment examine their notion of world peace. It stands as a kind of upper limit to political activity – compared to the lower limit, which is their collective emotions and feelings. In either direction one goes as far as one dares. The risk in both cases is the loss of popular appeal, which means loss of identity. Or perhaps one has even gone beyond this. The minimum requirements for international war after all are the desire to assert one's opinions beyond one's boundaries and an organized resistance to such a desire. Once cynicism and relativity of all values sway their minds, so that opinions, not to say convictions, are tacitly proclaimed to contain merit only for a moment and never justifiably for anyone except the individual who first stumbled across them – in short once They agree to disagree in order to protect each other's lack of organic brain, a war based on ambition or on ego is ruled out. Civil wars on the other hand occur in reaction to instituted authoritarianism. The desire to control exclusively, however, stems from a fixed belief in one's right to power (or rather to might, since power is the ability to do good) and such a belief is moral, whether sound or corrupt. Even corrupt morality, however, depends to some degree on the notion that something of oneself exists after death. The last vestiges of corrupt morality are still with us for a time, but rapidly the sense of time as a thing discontinuous in its very nature displaces and overrules it. Institution of any kind and by any power is doubted in its essence. One steps back and withholds one's commitment, since reason itself has become suspect. Vaguely demonstrative gestures are therefore all that remains of civil war if we scan the possibilities. As to revolutions and other upheavals of a circular nature, they have always required, as their springboard, an established historical past. Where can we find that today? The value of the past as such is seriously questioned. For the source of energy one relies on material sensation rather than on accumulated experience. The last revolution boils down to a self-satisfied indulgence in showmanship held together by a feeble thread of red menace, and the professional senility which was overthrown sprouts anew in the youthful bearers of the banner, this time as instinct rather than intellect. The only reality of world peace is therefore that times do not any more change. To speak economically, one has experienced the inflation of rights and the devaluation of the individual, while currency in itself has become meaningless.

We must ask what motivates those whose task it is to see that justice is done. The office of the law, while it exists, is beyond reproach, and surely this needs no repeating. In order to distinguish between the office and him who holds the office, integrity is required and ordinary humility. If the office of the law is abused, injustice is done. If the office of the law is allowed to stand but removed from application, a very peculiar phenomenon may be observed. In order to understand it, we should be reminded that the mere letter of the law can be separated out. One is left with logic devoid of sense. Human sincerity avoids this at all cost. The intellect however, when swayed by guile, attempts it, and with the help of a ruthless resentment it succeeds. It is this resentment which makes the difference between justice and what must be called wildness. In its early stages, resentment arises out of an unwillingness to endure. It is aggravated and becomes direct when forgetting and forgiving, as faculties, are consciously rejected. The slightest injustice then renders it chronic. One cannot overestimate the damage perpetrated by resentment that has run amok. It constructs, like a growing cancer, its anti-system of contorted values and inverted qualities, so that an entire substitute-view of life emerges which feeds on sheer madness and insanity. But it does so conveniently under cover. The mere appearance of legality provides this cover. Gratitude is utterly unknown. Cynicism has surpassed itself, and a glib, totally morbid fatalism sets in, openly opposed to practical sense, in the name of futuristic panaceas; and these are often adopted as attractive because they feign a ruthless practicality and reality of their own, and they tend to fascinate simply because they do not pander to the corrupt sentiments. Justice in these cases is negatively applied. One judges all that which is mortal to be irrelevant and dispensable in comparison simply to its absence. And this absence of mortal things is weirdly envisioned in terms of the ego, so that change itself is viewed as tending towards nothing; and this is understood to be the course of universal law. Consequently one strives to participate in this law as if it really existed and amazing energies are set free only to consume themselves; and naturally to consume whatever is susceptible to their effect. Negative justice is not at all the same as injustice. Injustice can be perceived to be what it is. Negative justice is not open to perception. It does not even leave tracks. One is peripherally aware of it only by dint of the resistance which it elicits in the conscience. And this resistance leads absolutely away from it and entails the establishment of the truth.

Materialism as an approach to life teaches the merely outward qualities and values and presumes to set these up with mathematical accuracy and ideal exactitude as the system of thought and feeling which may be relied upon to remain stable and to last. The essential test of material ponderability is said to be definitive objectivity in terms of both space and time. It is taken for granted, not merely assumed, that abstraction can be an end in itself.

To rule in this case means to render the universe experimentally superfluous, so that nothing can be made to happen that is not right away self-explanatory in predictable, material terms. To be ruled, by the same token, means to be repeatable entirely as a function of divorced matter, so that the existence of any particular entity can be said to be really of no account. However we must understand what a thing this matter is to these devotees of materialism, who only in the rarest cases own up to their colour. Matter, to them, is anything which can be pointed out. The strength of the proof lies in the number of those who agree to it. One lives for the crisis. When it comes, one circumvents it. Semi-conscious trickery is the materialist's passport from experience to experience. He trusts he can always escape through the loophole of the transcendent mood. Moods are in fact his emotional coinage. He strives forever to arrange them in a pattern for quick reference in case of need. The complete materialist takes a sort of humble pride in his calling. His mission, he tells you, is to change the world, to the better, one increment at a time, and though he will never manage it all, with modest deference, what with him being only another grain of sand on the beach, his negligible contribution satisfies him, and he is a realist at heart. God bless the state that has such citizens. They fit so sanctimoniously well. In multitude They represent the picture of automatised humanity which hangs life-size in the dream-room of each and every one of their ambitious politicians. What a paradise of busy contentment: On holidays the great leader pays affectionate tribute to the starry-eyed fruits of his labour, and for the rest of his sweet time he observes in benign detachment from on high, theoretically fulfilled on hypothetical cloud.

Industry as an investment of human labour – or as an investment *in* human labour – has very little to do today with what the word industry in reality means. One sees how They generally equate industry with the machine. Technically, machines have been used since the beginning of historical time. It is not until very recently however that machines have actually come into fashion. And every fashion dictates its own proliferation. The industrial age, as it is sometimes called, is well over. What one attempts to face today are the autocratic demands and inexplicable claims which the established machine makes on everyone. But this cannot even be called a problem, since problems have solutions. It is something which can only be turned away from. When They consider their body to be a machine and then identify with it as with the thing beyond which They do not exist, there can be no hope for them. The mechanized body is idolized – and of course devoid of soul.

So we notice how the machine does not any more lighten the workload for them but instead it drains them of the desire to better themselves, through discipline and diligence, and a languor sets in, a fatigue-mechanism which robs them of all capacity for interest while They depend upon their stomachs. The reaction to this fatigue is greed and rapacity, and these wear themselves out due to the principle of necessary financial increase. 'Economy' today ordains the optimum improvement of what is called the living-standard. As far as They are concerned, this standard can rise forever. They always want more than They need and hence They never get even what They need, although meanwhile there is available an overwhelming surfeit of real possibilities. Labour is not any more even a necessity, but a sickness of mind and soul. They labour so as not to lose track of their individuality. They attempt to enforce this as a worldwide principle so as not to lose consciousness of their identity. Integrity They call it, when the emotions are paralyzed and feeling has ingrown. Sincere They call every attempt to live up to their projected appearances. Falsehood, in short, reigns supreme.

Their principle ambition, as we have said before, is to survive as pleasantly as possible in the absence of life. Two priorities are accepted to guide them in their course. They wish not to harm, hurt or injure anyone, which generally means that They do not wish to appear to harm, hurt or injure anyone; and They wish to do no wrong and not to be wrong, which usually means that They do not wish to seem to do wrong or to be wrong. Hence They act as if They were doing right, which amounts to the criticism of wrong in others, and They behave as if They were helping, which amounts to performing ceremonies of help to gain them recognition by others. For to them, good is the absence of evil, and more correctly the outward (really the outside) absence of evil. Good as a substance in itself does not even outrage them any more and They do not any more search for stones because conveniently enough it occurs to them that good cannot really exist. In the past, sects have arisen devoted to the organized escape from reality. Today cults spring up in celebration of the fact that the escape has succeeded. Societies meet in order to pool their findings with respect to the actual absence of reality. Movements start in enthusiastic confirmation of the sensually and often sensationally proven belief that God is nothing and therefore cannot be unpleasant. Their survival is comforted by the fact that Christ does not know them.

Without rules They are lost because They are forced to fall back upon themselves. The first rules are always invented in order to slow down the process of self-recognition. More rules are fabricated in the hope of making self-knowledge impossible. Finally rules are manufactured in order to assure that real humanity can never again become a threat.

Rules themselves are in fact very useful and valuable for a time. Not to disobey them has always been in one's best interest. Here we are not concerned with their true value however, since rules are never made for the sake of their true value, and because we are interested in those who actually come up with them in the first place. Their purpose in doing this has been mentioned above. We know that whatever is good or true, whether it is action, behaviour or simply existence, is never in fact contrary to rules. Whatever is based upon rules however, or in actual accordance with them, or even in line with them, cannot be good or true,

The reasons which are commonly given for the existence of rules are order, convenience, and above all discipline. There must be rules, it is said, or else we live in anarchy. Rules keep away all that is anti-social, such as brutality, crime and violence. And rules are supposed to teach that no one can do just as he pleases.

It is on purpose that we make no difference here between laws and rules, since They choose not to understand the conditional justice inherent in laws themselves, but They take notice only of that aspect of the law which suits their principles of survival. Laws, rules and regulations therefore mean essentially the same to them, which is constraint on others and ease for themselves. It amounts to the same whether They rule or are ruled.

When They speak of the world, what do They have in mind? Let us attempt to put it into popular terms. First of all They point to all the things around them. Then They will tell you about everything that involves and preoccupies everyone like themselves. All this has no inherent stability or longevity of its own for them, and whether or not it becomes, quote: a better place to live in, unquote, depends entirely on themselves, on this virtue in this place at this time, and then on another virtue at another place at some other time, and the appropriate virtue comes from them, who are part of this same world; so the world is responsible for itself, and it controls itself or lets itself go, and whatever is not part of this puzzling complex is either crazy, or an enemy, or a Martian. Of course it may be all three at once. One can only marvel, how can such utter isolation and rejection sustain itself? However the illusion of continuance and of contact is in fact sustained – by rules. They form the spider's web in which all are equally caught and tied up. Equality itself, that idol of ideality, points only to these fetters which all have in common. What They call freedom on the other hand means secretly no more rules and blatantly more rules than enough, because They invent ten rules to get rid of one. They delight in such metaphysical conundrums as war for the sake of peace, revolution for the sake of fairness, tranquility for its own sake.

They refuse obstinately to distinguish clearly between the world and the earth. For most of them the two are the same. The one rule which helps them along here is the prohibition of financial dependence. Insofar as the world tends to centralize and to encourage a single point of vision, They are drawn each to his or her own concern at the exclusion of others. The earth by comparison is a confined territory and it is tempting in terms of merely outward material possession. Hence it seems logical to view the earth and the world as one so as to gain one's end more quickly. The mind of course must entertain this end as the possibility of ultimate omnipotence in terms somehow of selfishness. In short, one wishes to reign supreme, even if it means being the only one left. Whether by instinct, by intelligence, by the will or the feelings, or by any of the other human faculties, selfishness strives to establish itself to that end. The details of the effort may be petty or grandiose, laughable or fanatical, They do not mind, as long as They are able to take another step back in that direction. The rules They insist upon most are always in relation to their weakest defence against reality. The hypocrite will attempt to legalize morality. The fierce liar worships correctness and idolizes the law. By the rules They pursue you may know their character. Those who react against rules, who mock and spit at them – not those who break them but those who take it upon themselves to do away with them – these are a recent breed. They are either too clever for their own good or else incorrigibly obtuse. Their heads are full of anti-rules, and frequently They consider themselves to be intellectually superior. The axes They grind are disillusionment, reactionary hedonism, criticism, and others of that ilk, and They grind until the head of the axe is gone, whereupon They beat each others brains out with the handles.

The difference between the sciences and the arts according to Them lies solely in their application. And the nature of this application is in any case wild. In the beginning their scientist is conditioned in terms of a set of petrefacts and routines which he calls principles and laws. He is recognized as a great scientist while he manages to remain conscious of the temporary applicability of these principles and laws, and he is hailed as a genius if he strives, in spite of this consciousness, to come up with the law or principle which sums all the others up, thereby rendering them superfluous. It never strikes him that if he succeeded, he would have rendered himself superfluous, not only as a scientist, but as a man. This is so because these petrefacts and routines are always thought to explain reality and to control nature, when in fact they efface nature and obfuscate reality. The mistake is easy to understand. Nature, quite naturally, is always in growth. This implies unpleasant sensations and renewed mystery. The mystery is meant to be absorbed, resulting in clarity, and the sensations are meant to be suffered and endured, resulting in knowledge. The scientist who should have aided these processes, instead chose not to belief them in the first place, but rather to attempt the total annihilation of the unpleasant sensations themselves and to deny the emerging mystery out of hand. Studied annihilation and insistent denial, both of nature and of reality, are the mainspring and ambition of what is accepted by Them as science. Let us give an example, The scientist notices, most likely in experiment, an unusal event. He does not ask why he noticed this particular event rather than another, which would lead him to himself as a man, but holds this unusual event against a background of events that are familiar to him insofar as he has fitted them into a familiar pattern. The familiarity in both cases is conditioned by his own past behaviour, but he blithely leans on it, builds on it, and manipulates the unusual event accordingly. Whatever does not fit into the old pattern is treated as potential revelation, or else the pattern is adjusted. In any case the scientist never steps out of his own subjective individuality and he does not enlarge his objective identity. This identity therefore shrinks and his individuality passes away from him. It is only on the basis of such regression that one scientist can agree with another. If no two scientists could agree, in any single discipline even, there might be hope for them, but while they agree, for the sake of the academy or for the purpose of an objective body of science, to that degree do they labour towards their own banal end.

The world as such has never progressed. This has always been the bitter pill which only a few would swallow. It has not progressed, and was never meant to progress, since the world exists and has existed for the sake of reality, and reality progresses and always has progressed, by dint of the world or in spite of it. The end of the world simply implies that reality has no more use for it. As the world is discarded, so are all those who are part of it of course, even as logic dictates. It is interesting, though not surprising, that the world cannot be aware of its own surcease, and that it cannot be conscious of its cessation, since awareness and consciousness, insofar as they are part of this world, must naturally pass away at the same rate and time. But They assume that They can be part of the world and at the same time observe it, as impartial bystanders. This too is not surprising, for the definition of the world has always stumbled over this strangely narcissistic reflection of the world by itself, a continuing self-delusion until no world is left.

Science, at one time, dealt usefully with what could then be called the outer life, by interpreting and explaining it in terms of the inner life while that inner life was intact. Today those we mean in this essay can hardly even distinguish between an outer and an inner life. Such a distinction strikes them as fanciful and trumped up. By the same token we know that art could at one time repair and fortify the inner life, always on the grand scale in a preparatory fashion; and in order to succeed, this inner life had at least to be viewed as originally and definitively distinct from the outer life. Today, even as science openly devotes itself to the search for a foundation for the outer life alone on its own terms, attempting to interpret and explain the inner life in terms of this, so does art attempt to base itself on the outer life alone, and to sacrifice the inner life for this futile end. The artist looks upon it as a necessary evil that now and then he cannot but do without rules. He is called a good artist if he can remind Them somehow of the nonsense They have been forced by circumstance to discard, and he is hailed as a great artist if he can somehow include those circumstances. Let the artist play it by the book, They say, because then we know what he is on about; and some say, let him throw away the book, because then we know that he knows what he is on about; it all depends on whether They like what They like or whether They do not like what They like, and in this They are all alike, that They prefer to be bound by appearances. The artist knows that appearances need not be true in order to be temporarily pleasant, and so he helps himself to his slice of the cake. For the sake of these little pleasures he flatters and is agreeable, or he shocks and aggravates, or he stimulates and compromises, or he titillates and ruminates. Personally he cares about whether he fits in or does not fit in, and so he abides by the rules or else rebels against them, according to whether he is frightened or bored. The audience on the other hand knows that something need not be unpleasant in order to be good, and so they help themselves to their slice of the cake. Often they must first be purged of their conscience, which is called not beating about the bush, which is accomplished via the mere appearance of malice, cynicism and sarcasm; and once the conscience is drugged – carry on with the happy ending, with the social doctrine, with the asocial or antisocial doctrine, with the meaningfully understated fade-out, or with the experiment in aestheticism. Above all let no one try to set the real example, because that may not be for or against the rules. Back through history we see the pendulum swinging to ideal beauty on one side and to carnal beauty on the other. Lately this pendulum has stopped. The ideal is unbearable and the carnal is insuperable. The only way out is abstraction – methodical, hypothetical or theoretical. Even the technique, the mechanisms of human faculty, are coerced into abstraction. And there it sits and remains. The path to the concrete reality is damnably obstructed by the wish to rule and by the wish to be ruled.

Those we are dealing with primarily in this book have proverbially had their reward. Literally They are concerned only with their past and with what has been their due. The notion of time has meaning for them only as disagreeable interruption. Space they view in terms of private utility and public exploitation. Their basic weaknesses are the need for necessity, which They give in to in what they call a sense of duty, and the desire for feeling, to which They give vent in the name of what They call love. Both of these weaknesses are typical perversions. We know that only a very few things are necessary and perhaps only one. We understand that whatever is really necessary is by the very cause of this of the nature of a prerequisite. Insofar as it is necessary it cannot be an end in itself. It has nothing to do with life as such but rather with the preparations for life and the antecedents to it. One might say that it does not contain life, but certainly its promise. Therefore it must be, that without true hope this necessity becomes commonplace and stale. But the risk of great disappointment does not any more exist, and this is why They avoid hope. Their reasoning goes that since They have given up trying to win, They cannot lose. It is a sly reasoning and based on material calculation. It does not need to be practiced daily, because readily it turns into a routine and right away into a bad habit. The brain is immobilized and the soul sinks into a stupor. The mind accentuates its capacity for control at the expense of mastery, and finally the mind insists on control, at its own expense. The stoic bent is of this nature. The puritan persuasion embraces it. All war and military conflict is justifiable only to the extent that it is a reflex effort to break out of this self-imposed hopelessness. Here lies the answer to the contemplative question with regard to the possible justification of war. A reflex, yes; and at the same time a true effort. The effort must be potentially virtuous. To the degree that the motive stems from one's state, condition, situation or circumstance, it is not virtuous but fierce and its consequence is immoral and destructive. If the motive however arises conscientiously, out of care and concern for one's inner generation, there can be no breach of trust, and to the degree that merely outward reaction is avoided, the conflict results in hope regained.

Their usual behaviour however, once hope is gone, is actively to resist each and every attempt to shake them out of their torpor. It is in this resistance that their sense of duty resides. By moral and ethical camouflage They put each other off the scent so that the work of resistance can go on unhindered. One can watch this only in utter amazement. Since the virtues which might bring back hope are to be carefully and scrupulously avoided, and since curative influence must be put off guard, these virtues are meticulously labeled, lip-service is paid to them, ceremonies and cults of responsibility and principled intention are performed, and sincerity is the label for the willingness not to give the game away. The man who first stumbled upon what he called the collective unconscious little realized that it might have been smarter to let sleeping dogs lie. One cannot overestimate the tenacity with which They cling to their hopelessness. Eventually They even throw their precious self-esteem into the bargain.

A prepossession with privacy characterizes, as one would expect, their approach to death. They withdraw into a shell of non-concern. Perhaps, They feel, if we duck, it will go away. Consequently They virtually trip over their organism and stumble into the grave. The heart fails. There is a catastrophe of the brain. The soul, if any is left, goes out like a dim spark. The mind revolts against the burdensome body and in its attempt for autocracy it is annihilated. Usually, towards the end, this perverse sense of duty turns into a program of moral blackmail. States of submissiveness and moods of helplessness are feigned, there is a great show of flattery, confessions are trumped up, self-justification is pitifully indulged in, and all this for the sake of generating in others a response of care and charity, and if it is given, They use it to fire their selfishness.

We have described this weakness as a need for necessity. This is not to be mistaken for a choice of necessity. One may choose the necessary for the sake of eventual freedom. Reason might dictate such a choice. However to need necessity means to avoid choice because of the security-risk. One is so accustomed today to look upon a need as a subconscious, almost preternatural dictum of fate before which one is helpless, in other words as superstitious instinct, that it is treated customarily as a taboo. When one of them says: I need you! the conscious volition of the other one collapses, he gleefully throws all responsibility to the wind and gives himself over either to corrupt foolishness or else to egotistical escape. It comes as a surprise perhaps that under the charade of care and carefulness the common denominator is revenge. This has to do with the taboo of needfulness which They want to inflict upon each other. A taboo is a set of rules which not only defy analysis, but they are meant to put off even the approach of the senses. As long as no one questions the bare existence of the taboo, it thrives quietly, its complexity tending towards spoiled vision and its inexpressibility approaching utter ignorance of anything reasonable. The taboo renders stupidity exclusive. Intentions of revenge are therefore aroused when attempts at communication are suspected. The taboo is the idol of privacy and it negates communication. If it cannot succeed by the ordinary means of pretended agreement and fake compromise it switches over to publicity. No one is allowed to pry, and if anyone insists, everyone else is told something entirely different. Publicity is the technique of getting ahead of inquiry by producing false tracks; I pull your leg before you can push me into a corner. In the case of publicity the idol is generally called the image. In any case, revenge is inflicted, especially when They are nice to each other. Given half a chance They will work themselves up into fits of niceness, to safeguard the conventional taboo while They punish its enemy.

Their other weakness we have called the desire for feeling. It does not matter one whit to them what They feel, as long as They feel something. Pleasurable feeling of course is preferred, but even pain is better than nothing. For feeling to remain sound, as we know, honesty and integrity of purpose are the least requirements. When our feelings are not even screened by a kind intelligence They turn sour and fall apart. Mere feeling, which is neither guided nor led, gives one the illusion of being related while the actual relation breaks down. This break-down is feared by Them, however the possibility of a working relation in truth is feared even more. In fact it strikes their hearts with terror. They sense that They are caught. The only way out They see for themselves is to intensify as much as possible this illusion of mere feeling without purpose or reason, and this intensification quickly turns into a desire. They project it towards each other and focus it on themselves. They become experts in pinpointing the tiniest opportunities for its application, and when it happens They ruthlessly call it love. Energy of any sort is prized out of hand, being the fuel for this intensity, for this desire. Without energy, rot sets in. While it lasts, it is called affection. The affectation of this affection They call charm. The energetic affectation of charm They call charisma. None of it leads anywhere except to socially acceptable insanity, and in itself it may be summed up as the convention of respectable madness.

The grand master of the puppet show we are describing may be called quite precisely the spirit of the world. One might as well refer to it as a spirit because it moves without being moved. Far be it from us to call it evil. But even further be it from us to call it good. So why should we bother with it at all? Why not simply forget about it? Because it does not let us. Given the tiniest flaw in our system, it finds this out and makes war upon us in one way or another. And by now even the most worldly wise begin to suspect that their system is not perfectible. The solution of course is to scuttle one's system. What system am I talking about? It is the sum-total of all your attempts to do the world one better. You did get a glimpse once of how the world moved and it charged you with envy. If only you too could make things happen like that, a fortunate push of the absent-brained button and the ego enlarges by some sublime remote control. Perhaps you decided to make a little study of this seemingly all-powerful spirit. With every trick you learned, ten new ones seemed possible, so that the glory of it all shook you to the marrow. Then the time came to apply some of these tricks yourself. They who were around you told you that you had grown up, matured, entered into manhood or womanhood. Off you went, into your circle of like-minded acquaintances, on your career of admirable endeavour, and then you had learned the ropes, seen through the guiles and wiles of your supposed betters; in short you had established yourself in the world. Your reflection respected you and you paid the necessary tribute unflinchingly. Then the worm started to nag.

You were forced to take stock. Something somewhere seemed out of place, out of context. Now that They admired you, you despised especially them. The palpability faded out of your success. The more you held back, the more did your public urge you on. You closed one eye and called it your duty to give in to them. After all, They deserved you. Your family disintegrated. You closed the other eye. A man who serves the world must not be fettered by personal considerations. A young competitor stole your thunder and you were never heard of again. The graveyards are full of you. You have amounted to nothing.

The backbone of life for you was the daily routine. You carped and complained about it, and cursed it roundly. Or you clung to it carefully, for it made up your mind for you on many matters. Or you rebelled against it successfully, but your chaos needed it for definition. Never once did you live one whole single day, because you existed in fragments. Whether you rushed or stole along, finality frightened you and thoroughness displeased you. The occasion of your own end you held in contempt, and so you shrouded it in a vague religiosity or else dismissed it out of mind. Mood after mood assailed you. Either you fought back and the sap went out of you, or you gave in and turned soft. It seems that there was no way out for you even from the beginning. Eventually the strife dies down, you vegetate for a few moments, and then you pass away. One almost suspects that you have never been.

The spirit of the world dictated that They remained in their nature adolescent. It cherished and flattered them until by some accident, usually scandalous, They had come to taste from the tree of knowledge. Sweet as it tasted, exceedingly sweet, They would not understand the nature of that taste, and addiction set in, so that the repetition of trial and failure left ashes in the mouth and poison in the heart.

Once the spirit of the world has made its final appearance, it recedes and we claim its territory. They are suddenly left without their semi-conscious guide, and of course They have long forgotten that They fabricated him themselves, under false pretension, so They are forced to become aware of their utter helplessness. This is where we come in. The truth is of course out of the question. We must be false for the sake of the truth, deceiving without being deceivers. Those who we are understand this well enough. We do not give our support, but we lend it, and They in turn do not hinder us but go quietly about their business until their necessity runs out. What do we gain by claiming this territory? We can only mention it here. We gain our absolute self-sufficiency. A certain amount of house cleaning is required. The former inhabitant was a bastard. We are sons. Now our field of activity is entirely in our hands.

Not to rule and not to be ruled does not mean that one is slavish or unruly. Creation, we must remember, precedes chaos and anarchy, which are due to the foibles of man. Nothing exists prior to the Creator. The absence of the rule therefore does not mean chaos, and absence from the rule does not mean anarchy, but revolt against the rule means both. We know that the rule is to our advantage though we follow quite a different master.

To anyone who would be guided by the spirit of the world I would say: The will to conform is as absurd as the will to fame. And don't tell me that it depends on what you conform to or what you are famous for. The fact that you want these things is enough for me. Who are you performing for? What is your code of conduct? Why do you follow or observe a code of conduct? Because otherwise you would fall out with reality? Have a heart!

But let's face it, once you've spent your money you've got nothing left. Not that I expect you to agree with me. Your view of your life is complete to you and unshakable. Therefore I waste no time arguing with you. If only I keep your picture clear before my mind all goes well. It is a picture composed not even of appearances, but merely of mere appearances. Its outline is that of a bottomless pit, being rather the contour termination of the established ground. When I look at you, my eye adjusts to this bottomlessness and reflects upon itself. That may be a useful exercise, but I do not need you to make it possible or to bring it about. When I listen to the noises you make when you think you are speaking, my ear withdraws and concentrates upon its own hearing. Walk up beside me and momentarily my flesh creeps before my awareness of good sense is intensified. All in all, since these things have become true, you, my friend, have become dispensable. Now and then I act as if I were speaking to you simply to keep myself clean.

An effulgence moves into your place which I dare not name here. Suffice it to say that it fills us with absolute trust in each other. We have taken from you all that we need to take. You may go on your appointed way.

Those who would rule today must be based on the principle of world-wide acceptability. Their means on the other hand must stem exclusively from within the domain of their rule and from nowhere else. Thirdly They must be motivated by nothing except trust. Let us discuss these three: the principle, the means and the motivation. They have to do with the three questions respectively, pertinent to rule, of what, why, and how.

If we wish to rule Their affairs, it makes little sense to-day to employ high-sounding phrases to do with justice, fairness or equality. By this I do not imply that justice, fairness and equality are necessarily in the mouths of hypocrites, but I wish to emphasize the more useful approach under present-day circumstances. Let us look at Them as They are today, at what They are capable of and at what They can never be capable of as far as we can in all reasonable likelihood expect. First of all we must not expect Them to change in any particular direction. If They do change, we treat Them accordingly, but we cannot set out to change them either by force or persuasion of rule. This does away with all and every ideology. Again we remind that rule has to do with Them and not with man, mankind, or men. We are concerned here with Those of the world. They have an inclination and a tendency to death on one hand, and on the other hand They resist everything and anything that can do them good. No, this does not mean a death-wish, whatever that is, or that They are evil or insist on evil. They do not prefer to die. That would imply an awareness of death, which They prefer to reject. They are simply afraid for this life of theirs, and at the same time their nature draws them towards their death. Once we understand this we refrain wisely from attempting to rule out by any means this natural bent. It is as natural to Them as is digging to the mole or magnitude to the elements. Interfere with it and it carries on more acutely in another direction. It does point out to us however that any applicable rule must in fact point in a direction precisely opposite to this natural bent, and in terms which are entirely divorced from it. The slightest suggestion to Them that their nature, no matter how foul it is, might be even impinged upon, either sets them into an uproar or enslaves them in their faculties. Now the direction which is entirely opposed to this natural bent is natural survival. They wish to survive, and this is their greatest wish indeed, however They have absolutely no natural gift or talent for it at all, and the more They try, the more successfully do They die. The principle of acceptability therefore dictates that the rule must point positively in the direction of survival, with no reference at all to Their mortal nature. Since They do not recognize anything absolute, their survival of course is entirely relative, meaning that They do not wish to live, but to exist for longer.

The other aspect of this principle, as we stated above, is Their resistance to anything that can do them good. Our first impulse of course is somehow to break down or remove this resistance. But here again we would be tampering with Their nature. The resistance is not a tendency or an inclination, but an urge or a drive. A good influence reminds Them of their inherent shortcomings, and a good effect brings home to them their intrinsic imperfection. They wish to be good, but They do not know how to go about it. Their nature rebels against anything unpleasant. Hence They follow and give in to their urges and drives, and since these are natural to them, They do themselves only injury and harm. The humanitarian approach is therefore ridiculous. The rule may not impose anything good upon Them, since that hardens them in their errors, and it must not attempt to overcome any resistance to such good influence, since They would react as to an insult to their nature. The rule must instead open up to Them the essence of the conflict between their own natures and wishes, so that They are able to act out this conflict for each other and for themselves, but intentionally rather than accidentally. We must not expect them to understand the ultimate reason for their intentions as we have described it here, but They will notice the pleasure and satisfaction as They usually do. The rule only has to make the essence of the conflict available; They will take care of the rest themselves. They will consider it both as their duty and as their right to cultivate their own allegory, which is to say the allegory of themselves. We can interpret this allegory for ourselves; we are able to see how it reflects Their states, and how it corresponds to Their being; but They cannot understand this, nor are They able to find out. They are like fabricators and audience at once of a play that is unknown to them. Themselves They see only as possessors of rights and as doers of duties. Perform your duty, They tell each other, and your reward is pleasure; and They say: know your rights, keep them and insist upon them, and your reward is satisfaction. Pain and frustration They continue to view as negatable punishment.

Before we go any further we should bring to mind here that all Their rule is and must remain ironic to the last. We do well therefore fully to develop our sense of irony and to understand absolutely the process of irony itself. It arises out of a desire for mutual benefit by a superior intelligence when direct credibility cannot be achieved. When no credibility at all can be achieved by other means we use irony, in the case of language for example, by making possible and bringing about a relative monolog in response to us, and we do this by projecting our faculties temporarily to where we wish the monolog to take place. Our single concern is for the natural consequence of a set of circumstances to be made plain where a natural inhibition prevents that consequence from taking place. Clearly irony is the only sensible point of view when faced with ignorance that has established itself on the basis of a right of habit, and it is the only way to proceed when our certainty holds out longer than some approach which contradicts it. The ironic approach separates the contradiction which faces it into natural elements on one side and true elements on the other. The ironic operation allows the latter to go their own way while it orders the former for the sake of their own intrinsically caused operation. The ironic conclusion then unites the result of that relative operation with the elementary truth by way of intelligent reflection. They will always mistake appearances for the things themselves. They do this so totally that the time has come when even under duress They are unable to compare what seems with what is. This makes it difficult sometimes to take them for more than appearances themselves. But irony bridges the gap, until it no longer does good to bridge it.

We have mentioned above the principle of acceptability with respect to Their rule, and we have discussed it in terms of their mortal bent and with reference to their resistance of any potential benefit. This gave us an indication of what this rule must amount to. We turn now to the question of how it may be implemented and brought into operation.

We have said that the means must come from within the domain of the rule. Primarily this domain entails the content or stuff, not the form in any way, of Their behaviour. When They compete with each other for the sake of financial gain, for example, the content of that behaviour is guile and materialistic increase, and the stuff of it may be greed, or vanity, or murder, and money. The form of it on the other hand may be mercantile, capitalist, communist, businesslike, military and so on. Secondarily this domain is made up of all that They believe to be related to them, and especially of those supposed relations. We may refer to this as myth and the study of it as mythology.

What interests us about the content of Their behaviour is that it can in no way be understood as a function of will and intellect, as an expression of thought and feeling or in terms of the emotions and passions, but that it must be viewed entirely as a function of itself, as an expression of itself, and in terms of itself. In short, it will not be explained and remains inexplicable. The rule we have in mind therefore must adapt itself appropriately. It may not give evidence of a purpose, goal or end that is in any way essential, and it must be self-explanatory to a fault. In other words it must be so immediately obvious that it will be taken as if for granted. Enforcement of the rule therefore comes to lie within the framework of popular custom, so that he who goes against the rule does not infringe upon or break some particular social or moral code, which might allow him to exchange one clique for another, but he diminishes his supposed credibility in itself, so that anyone and everyone will naturally find it more difficult to assume his individuality or to come to terms with his identity. It is not the case then that those of more similar opinion find it easier to overlook a breach of rule in each other then those of more contrary persuasion, but it happens that the exact opposite is the case. The breach of this rule quite simply dissembles the faculties, and where an illusory agreement exists, any risk to its apparent foundation is viewed with trepidation, while in the absence of such agreement apprehensiveness deepens and general mistrust is increased. It is therefore in their interest as individuals to observe this rule, rather than being in their interest with respect to others. And They are all the same in that They value above all else their individuality.

As far as Their domain of relativity is concerned, we may think of it as being generally composed of sympathies and antipathies, all of these being based upon temporary appearances of the materialistic order. They are related to others like them for example insofar as They stem from the same bodies, and a body is a sufficiently similar appearance of flesh. They understand one thing to be related to another when the two of them have a third thing in common, and this third thing must be held together by the other two. For the rule to have meaning here it must seem to demonstrate a universal duality without actually doing so, and this duality must appear to be unified without really being so. In short it must impress upon Them a fictional oneness. Hence we speak of rule due to the will, or willed rule, and of rule according to the intellect, both of which have to do with the wished rule. This requires some further explanation. The difficulty lies in the impossibility of a singular viewpoint. Naturally enough we do not in truth wish to rule, but regard it rather as an expediency for the time being. Hence only an aspect of our wish plays a role in this activity. So it is also with the will and the intellect. Then again we cannot give another name to that particular aspect of our wish, since that would divide us against ourselves. When we speak of rule due to the will or according to the intellect therefore we keep in mind this partiality of our concern. – According to the intellect then this rule deals with states and situations. Their limitations and ends are carefully taken account of and clarified in terms of popular certainty. Due to the will, causes and motivations are defined in popular terms and brought into regular operation. In reference to our wishes, at the same time, Their individual concerns, with respect to themselves, each other and their environment, are taken into special consideration under the projected application of this rule. This takes us straight into a discussion of that third prerequirement for those of us who would rule today, which was stated previously, namely that the motivation must be nothing but trust. What we mean by trust must be described at the beginning. It has nothing to do with taking anything at face value. On the contrary, where They are concerned we may take nothing at face value. Remember that it is the rule which is to be motivated by trust, and not our behaviour in general, Outside of its effect on Them this rule has no meaning. So do not attempt to picture it abstractly. Neither can you imagine it outside of its process. They, as such, can be easily pictured or imagined, as long as one does not hope to achieve anything else by this. Once They have involved themselves in this rule, and so that this may come about successfully, we must trust Them insofar as this involvement has taken place. Initially we simply allow the rule to catch, so to speak, with respect to Their apparent presence. But here we do well to guard against the unreflected illusion that comes our way, especially in the case when They are 'nice'. Their presence only appears, and that appearance only appears, and so on indefinitely. Once the rule has caught on, certain positive elements are attributed to us, and we should not make the mistake of attributing these to Them. They originate with us and are given back whole, and it is idle curiosity that disturbs the reaction. These positive elements may be looked upon as the lower limit of the rule's application, and the upper limit is a show of intimacy. This intimacy soon enough conquers even the capacity for mere reaction, so that They are momentarily returned to their own nature, which permits the full effect of the rule.

The full effect of the rule is measured in terms of peace and welfare. We know what They mean by peace and welfare, and we know what we ourselves mean. While the rule is applied, these two meanings never come into conflict.

We can now speak more openly about the direct procedure of the rule. The parameters of course are not truth and goodness, but right and help. It is clear that They must have the right to get what They need. No one may take this away from them. But how is one to decide what They need? Enough to keep body and soul together? Obviously some single standard must be developed which makes sense to everybody and persuades without fail. To set it up we definitely need a sense of humour.

The standard of popular necessity which the rule implies must offer too much satisfaction for too little a price. While They feel less deserving than They are made to feel They are not afraid of each other. This is naturally very important. The standard is therefore based on mutual likeness. One of them is like the other and the other is like the one while the two are not like each other. In fact no two of them are like each other, but each one of them is like the other. This means also that They readily like each other. Let no man attempt to compare this to the bare truth. Out of this likeness arises the behavioural aspect of the standard. It is composed or made up of natural feelings, and its meaning is: I like you as much as you like me. Independent of any standard, the degree of liking ebbs and flows as it would, perhaps in line with the moon or mars, and each one takes credit nevertheless for manipulating fate, so that it was either a case of: I like you because you like me, or of: I will like you so that you will like me. But with this standard in position each one of them is allowed to collaborate in his own fate insofar as it involves pleasantly the fate of another. Hence They gauge their behaviour not any more in accordance with their own reactive faculties but according to a collective inter-reaction. On one hand They cannot any more affix labels to each other, whether nice or not nice, and on the other hand They show each other exactly what They are made of. Needless to say one cannot give another name to this standard, since it would quickly be isolated out of operation,

It is impossible for Them to interfere in anything that is not popular. They are tied to the apron strings of their popularity. Take it away and the identity collapses. Increase it beyond a relative proportion and the individuality gives way. Original authenticity in Them is a ghost in the past. So do not expect from them any positive contribution, no matter how clever you think you are.

Popularity is the great spider in the night. It spins the most complex webs of intrigue, in order to make you believe anything before you believe in yourself. They must ultimately always deal with their friends and acquaintances on a mercenary level, since They must all survive. Their blood-relations take a bit longer to shake down, because 'blood is thicker than water' but eventually They too are sifted through selfishness.

We defeat popularity by revealing ourselves not until we are well known. We behave as we want or wish to behave, depending upon our degree of perfection, but he who does the behaving is utterly concealed wherever that behaviour is met by even the slightest degree of ignorance or by even the smallest amount of ill will. However the absence of ignorance and ill will does not mean that we are well known. Ill will can simply pass away, without its opposite taking effect. Ignorance can disappear and there is no more knowledge than there ever was. In the face of the mere absence of these then we cannot reveal ourselves, but we may show ourselves. This does not lead to popularity, since it does not allow for an idol, and it does not lead to unpopularity, since it does not scandalize Them through their own errors, but it causes them to fall back upon themselves, Consequently their support comes to lie in exactly what They have managed to construct or build up until then.

They themselves, without popularity, initially take revenge upon themselves, by believing their own lies. Hence They must go through an actual stage of unpopularity. Their acquaintances seek out their company so as to shun them, or else They are spoken well of and at the same time avoided. Moral precepts cannot any more be employed to excuse or justify fault, and soon They attempt to pay men money for the least peace of mind. The best They can do however is to buy the absence and annihilation of their mind. Needless to say their body goes with it. But They will gladly empty their purses and relinquish their possessions if a man only accepts them, for when They give to men, the contract of right giving is at least not perverted. When all is given They prefer to labour and slave for their mental and physical deprivation if only They are protected from their faculties which must otherwise turn against them, until the time comes that They are no more.

They are strange, even to each other. When the pretence is over, the catastrophe sets in. It takes but a single word of truth, one sole occurrence of reality, and the tide of popular activity and passivity ebbs and flows no more.

What They call their world is based on money. Money means one thing in fact and another thing to Them. In fact money is a convenience and an expedient entirely with respect to trade. Surely one can accept that even paper money was brought into use for this reason. One state or country which uses a mode of exchange among many which do not: this presents a different problem to reason than the case of all countries of the earth using a mode of exchange. Without a mode of exchange such as money, trade must necessarily depend upon private value. I would like your bathtub, and unless you are willing to let me have it as a gift, a trade of some sort must proceed. But whether or not a trade can be possible depends in turn upon whether I have in my own possession something you would like to possess rather than your bathtub. Perhaps if I agree to paint your house you will let go of your precious tub. I tempt you with articles that are relatively of less worth to me, and you try to get as much out of the exchange as you personally see fit. In all honesty both of us stand to gain if the exchange of goods or services comes off. As soon as money is coined however, which has little or no value outside of its designation as a mode of exchange or trade, an assumption is made as to the value of the total amount of goods or services obtainable within a defined territory. Needless to say this assumption is never admitted. Now we do not speak of goods but of commodities. The *facility* has become the standard rather than *personal preference*. Public value has taken on a bogus absolution, and this means the traditional birth of mammon. There is no cause and effect relationship between the mode of exchange and mammon; the two really amount to the same thing. Keep in mind that we are dealing with Them and not with abstract theories or ideas. They believe and even insist that the world is finite and changeable by them. Their opinion of money is as of a fixed quality upon which They may base their survival speculations. They view their own wishes and needs in terms of such opinions and their morality grows out of them.

Money, in short, is their expression of their ego. The popular ego expresses itself as what They call their standard of living, which amounts to the world value of their unit of money. Sooner or later They all must accept that their standard of living has stopped rising. This is because the popular ego has finally been deflated, causing it, as it were, to ingrow, so that we do not any more speak of an ego but of socialism. Of course They are always more than one but socialists can occur one at a time. A socialist, mind you, is by no means an individual human being. Socialism differentiates Them negatively, so that They acquire a fictitious relativity. Hence the pseudo-religiosity of socialists. (We are not referring to a political creed here.)

There is also an art that is meant especially for Them, which does not tax their faculties unnecessarily but simply concentrates on their deliverance from themselves and each other. Since They need nothing beyond this, and since They cannot accept anything else, there is no reason for disturbing this life of theirs with the truth or for confronting it with reality. Art of this nature therefore deals with itself and only with itself, and always in terms of mere appearance. Its application is free entertainment. There is reason for it too, but this is not included in the art, because They would only be confused by it.

Mere appearance, as we know, is always both temporary and contemporary, and at the same time it can be pointed at and pointed out without changing or disappearing. Look at it long enough and associations of likelihood are fashioned which in turn take the appropriate appeal required at the current moment. Possibilities are of course not taken into account, and whatever happens hinges upon contradiction, negation and resistance, with an insistence upon death thrown in for good measure. Mere appearances are easily collated within some familiar frame of reference and organized according to the natural illusion which accrues to them. Only a hint at logic is required to open vast wells of confusion to quench the thirst for the great myth. They do not take an interest in anything, but They are interested in what interests them, and there is an end to it. They know what They like. The critic has a field day when he can see through everything and it reminds him of his glorious self. Acute vision for detail develops, combined with a distinct feel for subtlety. The brain leaps out into the open as it were and performs its specialties. Divine irony takes root in apparent particularities, and since it is the particular which ensnares its kin, one notices right away the effort to please and the intention to gratify, not to be confused with honest effort and sincere intention but allowed to nourish itself on its own illusion for the sake of satisfaction and good fortune all around.

Here we make an end to this book.

* * *

Jesus Today

*

essay

*

Traumear

*

What I wish to emphasize in this essay is that while we feel obliged, even tempted at times, to distinguish between Jesus-experience and messianic understanding, what matters is that time and again, by way of our creative being and doing, we make the two one. Nothing is to be gained from 'making a thing' out of Jesus-sentimentality and mere piousness on one side or of Messiah-theology on the other. The author therefore concentrates on this creative process, which he recommends as our response to those times when we find ourselves divided between head and heart, between spirit and flesh.

The essay was originally written in German, which accounts for some slight awkwardnesses in translation.

*

Jesus Today

We don't want to attract attention with our opinions among people. We want to enjoy ourselves in secret. However for some reason that doesn't seem to be allowed. Love sings its own self and will not allow itself to be tidied away, so that we understand as much about love as our practice of it brings home to us, not more. If at the moment I love, then at the moment I also understand love.

Jesus today is active in our loving and at the same time in our faculty of understanding. More accurately, he is active in the way we understand, in other words once again in the process, not merely in the faculty. So that we don't mistake Jesus, we understand lovingly and love with understanding, taking care not to let one of these separate off from the other. Both together make us human today in the way that Jesus requires as a minimum in us if he is to join us quite openly as Messiah.

What should I do and how should I behave, so that Jesus can be strong in me? Every thoughtful human being who is no longer content with an existence devoid of truth, or with a disembodied truth, asks himself this question. For in Jesus we promise ourselves the presence of an evolved human being, while nonetheless no one can point this contemporary being out to us. No one can say: "There he is" without lying. All the same he is currently present. How can that be explained? Or better, how does it come, that we feel we owe ourselves an explanation here? Who has told us, in all our modesty, that proofs are necessary even into the heart of time? What goes on at the moment must not always go on and our concepts, our ideas and opinions, advance well enough towards their goal so long as we occupy ourselves with them lovingly and with understanding. No one first has to withdraw us from time and point the finger at what is most essential. After all, everything is meaningful, only not the transient present, and in it we should find our wellbeing..

The transient, meaningless present is the realm of our loving understanding and of our understanding love, in which Jesus finds his way into us and shows up in us; where he does his work, being vigorously effective and in such a way, so that with the best of wills we cannot ascertain the difference between him and us - which does not particularly surprise me, because I know well enough how hard I tried in the past in order to get on with my ego-tistic business. I knew very well in those days where I wanted to get to, with my indolent ways in the face of my conscience and with my possessive ambition among people and human beings. I didn't much like it when somebody interrupted me in my driven existence and in my hopeful survival, for the time was ripe for me and I sensed that in my bones. Don't we all sense that, when love as the original source shows up in us and we cannot help ourselves but we just have to do as we do? Why should we after all still bother with the applause or the envy of the innocent bystanders who do nothing except guard themselves against any and every crisis.

*

In those days, in the past, I lost myself entirely in the love that appealed to me, and so can you. Some human beings understand love and they understand how to love and just as they observe you, so do they right away help, because they can see with that insight within, that is ready prepared for them messianically, how what counts for you is the fidelity of your behaviour in the present. You may be silly or temperamental, you refuse to participate in the transience of things, as if you believed you were invisible, or en-tirely without probability. Your behaviour as such draws you to the attention of those around you and you don't know how to side-track them. Surely there are some among those nearby who might care for you rather than merely pointing at you critically!

How fortunate you are, if only you knew it, because everything about you fits and makes sense. Be constant, smart. The god who deals well with you in himself, he is content with the fact that you are here and among us, though you may not understand. Theological observations and critical comments are not to the point here. Until now you have nowhere lived in the present, only always in the past or in the future, and out of those two you could make nothing except always only feelings and thoughts, and those became problematic. If at that time I had read to you these few lines, you might well have become truly aware, however clarity arrives only in the present, when we know what we know and when time no longer hinders us.

Why and in what way does time hinder us? This is difficult to answer. Perhaps nothing like time exists, except as a hindrance. And who is hindered? As a matter of fact only he who knows nothing of time except those sorrows that time, so to speak, sends and those felicities by means of which it more or less signifies. So we depend on time and fear it at the same time and are dramatically divided in ourselves. Do we know children who are still childlike and allow themselves to be hindered by time? They have to be schooled in that first. Let them be comfortably adapted to the clock and to the calendar and that is only as it should be. Only if we learn how to take time up into consciousness, are we then not hindered by it, which is no small thing.

Time bothers those who want to remain ignorant of it because they wish to live unhindered in the past and in the future, unpresent. Just then when they turn away from time, it disconcerts them. Otherwise they would get caught up in themselves like a scrap of sheep's wool on barbed wire, and even these chosen words would be of no help to them. What a pity, because in every one of these words the word lets us know of itself and the word never fails.

So not he who rids himself of time is successful in his being but only the companion of time, in whom all things become fugitive because he rebuilds it all. The companion of time, the contemporary one – him we praise. It is he who manages to adapt to the eternal.

*

Now we may assume there is a realm of the present in which the past and the future are reflected. Not everyone is able to search right away in his memory in order to find out how this is to be accepted. Often we suppose it all will continue for us as it has gone on so far and we do not necessarily let events have rights, even over our being. If it turns out that something happens, then let it accommodate itself to our sensibility, so that rather than being mastered by history, we will be the masters of it.

What we more or less call our history – let it play its role. Let us conveniently observe it and find it interesting. If it confuses us, we would rather it had kept our hands off it.

Jesus is today an event that confuses some of us.

Mind you, this we know already from our experience of carnal love, that things happen that confuse us, that shake us up and renovate us in a way. Does one ever become accustomed to the erotic? Is the sensual sex drive not triggered off in a trice? All else happens afterwards and depends on this and that, which is to say on education, on experience and on conscientious conviction. And oh how nicely and allegorically the erotic lends itself to our wish for renewal, this we may observe when we glance at the film industry; it senses well enough what people need and with what they allow themselves nevertheless to be satisfied, for a short time and a few dollars.

The rather crass opposition between spirit and flesh comes into prominence here and we intend to concern ourselves with it for a short time.

A supernatural sensibility is no longer open to us. It may well be the case, that now and again, out of fear, we attempt to squeeze ourselves into such an opening, on account of a lack of personal confidence. However we need to rid ourselves of the superstition that such a thing as this supernature, as anything supernatural in reality, can exist. What we call nature, that we must right away also call human nature; an immortal element has crept in here and we will never be able to rid ourselves of that, thank god; the supernatural is after all just such a hypothesis of what is supposedly the inhuman and the unnatural. We need to become clear in our minds about the difference between that which is spiritual and that which is supernatural. The so called supernature is of premessianic character and belongs into the past, where one waits for the coming Messiah or Son of Man and where one knows nothing yet of Jesus and still has no real experience of him.

The Jesus experience, as it happens, stands incontrovertibly between supernature on one side and subconsciousness on the other, and contradicts both. We may hold this fact fast in our mind because it explains many a thing.

The supernatural impulsion is therefore only one side of the problem – we fit ourselves into this problematic situation only because Jesus himself today is dear to us and not a post-modern grimace of the mass media. As soon as a messianic hope arises in the world, as for example in the late-Jewish cultural sphere, what also comes about, as an accompanying phenomenon, necessarily, is that particular sensibility due to which man similarly desires to depart from what is evil and deadly, however of a Messiah he wants to know nothing. That the experience of something supernatural begins in man only if at the same time the hope for the Messiah were to stand open to him, this makes sense to us, for god gives us what is good, however it depends on us what we make of it.

In the pre-messianic past then, the confusion about the supernatural was easily possible and likely, because right up to the time of the hope for the Messiah one could easily remain unconscious about one's humanity, if one particularly wished. And then, with the arrival of the messianic hope, it was even possible to choose the inhuman/supernatural. This abyss opened and one could leap in. That it was actually done, to this testifies Phariseeism, which did not exactly look kindly on the historic Jesus.

We take an interest in the premessianic history only so that our own time in comparison becomes more comprehensible.

Like a wedge this hope for the Messiah drives itself into human being, and as a negative accompanying phenomenon the supernatural joins the unnatural and – to the unconscious is joined the subconscious. Consciousness of god and hope for the Messiah then signify the positive, historic stream of time, which eventually becomes a tributary into the ocean of the Messianic realm, while on either side negative accompanying phenomena retain this stream of time in relief: in other words the unnatural/unconscious first, which then, more separated and forced asunder, appears as supernature and subconscious.

As soon as the messianic hope turns into the Messianic event, supernature as such is no longer possible and a subconscious as such is no longer possible either, since both phenomena belong into the premessianic time. They are no longer possible for human beings.

The education of man, so that he should become human, begins after all with god-consciousness, continues with the messianic hope and reaches its completion in the Messianic realm of god. We can speak of development only up to the beginning of the realm of god, then many a thing happens suddenly, in the wink of an eye. Whoever does not stand on solid ground then, drowns and whoever cannot handle the fire, burns. Tersely formulated, after the premessianic age, and as soon as our age is past, the elements stream into us and woe to him who is caught off-guard by them. The historic man of the past died but we, as men, women and children, we live, and we have eternal life.

Supernature and subconsciousness therefore do not stand open to us because we are eternally live, that is to say really and messianically living men, women and children.

Spirit and flesh: this emerges finally, under the messianic point of view, as one and the same. Only from here, from this complete, godly/human point of view, it occurs to us to ask how spirit and flesh were after all seen at one time as a duality. Do we not see now, however not until now, how this is one, visible and invisible? This great mystery is only then uttered with true lips when the messianic organ of sight finally also exists. We may well say we see many a thing, however we only see it halfway, "through a glass darkly", often addicted to prejudices and cleaving to appearances. Messianically one sees the same, whether one sees it as flesh or does not see it as spirit. One believes the same, whether one believes it as spirit or does not believe it as flesh. There are those who maintain that this secret cannot be expressed, but surely that was done just now. Naturally one has to know what this is about, otherwise one sees, outside oneself, paradoxes that actually lie in the eye, and from self-produced riddles one tries, on the same basis, to force a solution.

Flesh and spirit, then, is no antithesis. Until we ourselves have progressed through the god-consciousness and the messianic hope, however, and have arrived within the messianic event, we will not believe that these are not antithetic. But then that is what this is all about. In the absence of the Messiah, of the first real human being in spirit and flesh, we could not possibly arrive at a point where we believe this and have this insight.

So it cannot be right when someone says that for Jesus the kingdom of God was supernatural. Neither can it be right that in the late-Jewish cultural realm the messianic hope and the messianic expectation had supernatural character. Those who knew what they were saying and what they wrote always had an inalterable notion of the eventual positioning of flesh and spirit as one, and this as a possibility for the future and as the principle of the past, because they understood to what extent this final opening of eyes and ears could not but be brought about by god. Those of the supernatural and subconscious persuasion did after all know nothing except that dependency upon laws, angels and ideas.

Only look closely at the two sayings: "The kingdom of heaven is within and among you." and "You will see the son of man coming on the clouds of heaven in power and glory." In the former the exclusively inner realm is avoided and in the latter the merely outer likewise. Subconsciousness and the supernatural are merely referred to in terms of their coincidental rejection. They receive a harsh rebuff in that Pharisees and scribes are described by Jesus as hypocritical. The scribes did, after all, come up with the subconscious, just as the Pharisees invented supernature. In that Jesus rejects both as hypocrites, he openly declares his solidarity with the realm of god as flesh/spirit.

*

We now stand before the Jesus-experience itself, which nowadays is brought so expressly into the forefront; many a one knows it in person while others strive for it.

The event of the Messiah is not the life-experience of Jesus, we should be clear about that right from the start. Spirit is not flesh. Both, however, are one and the same.

That which has occurred does not necessarily have meaning for all, however whosoever wishes can take possession of this meaning and sense. Clearly, the messianic event is fact and occurrence that stands open and ready for all. With the Jesus-experience the opposite is the case. What I experience has import only for me but I can, if I so wish, render it useful and advantageous for some, for several and for many.

*

Where do we experience the live Jesus? In our hearts. Our heart is the organ of love, even as our eye is the organ of sight. And what we experience as live and not 'merely', is ours always, this we should remember.

52

Now, however, Jesus is lord in the god-realm whether we experience him in our heart or not. He is our lord and master whether we experience him or not. And because he is our lord and master, we live and we do not die, not because we have experienced him. We do well not to avert our eyes from the main issue, and the main issue is our live creativity and our real living in the god-realm which is ours and no one can take it from us.

I do believe this is the time when we should clarify what such a live experience (Erlebnis) amounts to. After all, our actual and eternal life, has, allegedly, nothing in common with experience. We only enter this sphere of life when we experience something and then we exit from it again. Meanwhile something about us has changed. Whoever can himself enter into this sphere of life, he did not live previously, and afterwards he lives only to the extent that he occupies himself with live experience and insofar as he completely comes to terms with it. It is possible to experience this or that and every time we do, something is borne into us, so that we can well speak of a burden and of a load. Every experience burdens us and we may find this burden onerous, so that we may try to shrug it off. Then, however we are not only rid of the burden but also of the life in connection with it, and this we ought to regret. Sadly we do it all too often however, that we readily enough experience but then we refuse the burden. At times we even curse the experience itself, on account or the apparently unavoidable inconvenience connected with it.

The Jesus-experience too is like that, in that a burden comes to rest on us; so we pleasantly enough experience the one who is life itself, only to reject him afterwards as too inconvenient. Both of these we feel right about.

Now we could say: A live experience consists of ordinary experience and achievement. What burdens us is the experience without the achievement. So the achievement is crucial. Whatever it is that carried itself into us now desires to be assimilated and set up in the world, or more correctly, in the realm. "Pick up your cross and follow me" says the historical Jesus, to those who genuinely wish to live. This burden, this cross, lies on us as soon as we experience Jesus, life itself, and then this load is huge and we may carry it throughout our life, while our achievements are our works that extend and deepen the god-realm.

In what way is Jesus life itself? Jesus today is Messiah, and devoted to us in all things. His inclination to us is spontaneous and barely comprehensible. The essential point, however, is that wherever he is, god as the father also is. And this implication and involvement of god is life.

I cannot imagine that. I am weary now and don't know what to do, because the burden of the day lies on me, so that I desire to rest and to sleep. Burden, however, implies achievement for me and if I am tired, then somewhere in me energy is available that has not yet been invested. So I make myself responsible for this tiredness and take it upon me instead of letting myself sink down beneath it. At the same time I carry on with this present task. Result: an achievement and liveliness instead of tiredness.

Jesus in my heart, that is an idea I suddenly have and I cannot help it. Can we experience life itself? Ideas arrive from god, are godly. That the godly bears itself into my heart, surely this should be agreeable to me. For that reason I call this an idea, because at first my head and my heart participate, even before I myself notice. An idea draws my attention to it, that happens automatically and then what is important is the realization of this idea, and for that I have need of my heart. I require courage for this, for this realization, heartiness, and whoever has not the heart for it, will find that this idea occurs to him as coarse while he becomes over-enthusiastic and ends up with an ideal and an idol. Organic love is missing, so that, in short, the godly sign, the idea, is abused and misunderstood by us and does not become a reality but an ideal or even an idol.

*

So we work towards the live Jesus-experience. Whoever has lost himself presumptuously in the idea of Christianity and even has striven towards, or even competed for, the most intensive and self-persuasive feeling of piousness (not the same as piety), and if he did it in accordance with his culture, his tradition or education, he may well have the most arduous task still ahead of him. And along with the feeling of piousness one should right away also mention the thought of a belief. In both cases the idea has not been realized but – eternalized. This eternalization of an idea is something most complicated and we do well not to fool ourselves into supposing that it might be useful to try to follow it up in all its sophistications and profundities. From the beginning it might be best to realize, that in this case we have to do not with an actual reality but with an idea. A brick is not a piece of wood, nor is it a tree. Then it has to be accepted that ideas are secondary to all realities, so that every undertaking to establish an idea as an independent thing (the contradiction lies in the word itself) must fail. Human beings rank superior to angels and laws serve the truth. {Angels, ideas and laws may, in this manner, be superficially compared. Angels point to our Jewish inheritance, ideas are of Greek origin and laws (not the law) carry a Roman reference – something like that}

However let's stay with ideas. If we observe how energetically the attempt of idea-eternalization is made throughout the centuries, we cannot but arrive at the fullest appreciation of how hugely difficult must be a courageous realization of an idea. Whoever is persuaded of the godly character of all ideas and is done with boasting of his own ideas, is already advantageously gifted. However he still lacks something that is just as important, namely the insight into the fact that ideas are essentially serviceable; that they minister to us. That whatever is godly serves and wishes to mister to us human beings and that such ministration is indispensable to us, this never readily enters our thick heads. Vehemently we argue against that, because do we not, after all, wish to go into raptures over our God and prostrate ourselves at His feet in the sand – while we fear that unless we behave like this, the next step is bound to amount to presumption. A psychic duplicity lies concealed in this. All too often we have burnt our fingers on account of some actual presumption and now we suspect we have a chance for redress, for a surrogate gratification and even for a renewed but clandestine presumption and we mendaciously hope to get away with it because we squeeze our eyes shut. However this sounds as if we did it intentionally and that would be unjust, for it happens to us, and always again because we do not – with a will – do the opposite.

Every attempt then – every temptation – to eternalize an idea, as an idea, works counter to our live experience of Jesus. We forfeit in this way every opportunity for realizing that idea (for fulfilling the law, for hearing the angel).

Now we are more than ready to call the live experience of Jesus the realization of the godly idea itself. For that we require fantasy and imagination. These two, precisely, as one can understand, despised and rejected by the eternalizers of ideas, here achieve their rightful goal, embodied and spiritualized.

We may understand here too how it comes that the path, from the duplicitous and inwardly contradictory eternalization of ideas towards a Jesus-experience must imply, for those idea-eternalizers, a falling-off and a relapse – in terms of atheism. In fact a thoroughgoing atheist may stand closer to a live Jesus-experience than a convinced and enthusiastic eternalizer of the idea, who intentionally labours under the delusion of a supernatural and subconscious God. By a thoroughgoing atheist I mean someone who rejects in one way or another both the supernatural and the subconscious – except that for him, of course, the danger exists, that he may stick obstinately to this rejection, becoming addicted to atheism, as it were, instead of simply letting the matter rest and working towards some realization of the idea.

In order for us to succeed with this realization, we need, as we have seen, courage and heartiness. In what way courage? Because we have to overcome something in ourselves and because we have to stand a test, which is required to show whether we are worthy of the undertaking or not. "Whoever sets the plough into the earth and then looks back is not worthy of me."

Let us speak of a notion, rather than of an idea. If something occurs to you, do you then right away behave or act in accordance with this notion? Not unconditionally. First you reflect. Then you weigh up. You count the cost. And that is quite right and proper. That makes the difference between the force of the idea and the embodied being or shape (Gestalt) of the idea. Whatever occurs to us does so forcefully. The essence or being of the notion, not its size, is forceful and with that we are to understand that we are not first asked for our consent. The godly 'falls' into the realm of our experience, (in German: notion = Einfall) without our having given our consent and this makes out the forceful character of every notion. Whatever notion 'falls into us' right away has being for us. Our agreement (or otherwise) comes afterwards. It depends human-naturally on us and we may courageously decide in its favour rather than playing the role of the victim who has been violated and is fabricating an –ism out of it.

We know of a preparation for all that occurs to us as notion or idea, and that is upbringing and education. We know that this is crucial when we observe what happens when notions land on bad soil.

The coming of Elias, for example, signifies, in the old-Jewish cultural realm, the preparation for what is forcefully godly. The evangelical reports point out to us how the god-idea itself falls forcefully into Jesus – and how he, prepared by the Baptist, decisively responds to it – even though, and because, it is forceful in character. Also we see how Jesus immediately embodies and spiritualizes it: notice the god-fatherly approval.

Upbringing and education as preparation for the godly as forceful notion or idea entering into us is therefore advisable. However then what counts is our willing consent to this forceful happening, and here we realize that a great deal needs to be caught up and rectified after the typical upbringing and education that someone is allotted nowadays.

Our consent to the idea, to the notion of the godly, makes it possible for the godly to 'shape' itself for us. That which is forceful stands, so to speak, in front of us and introduces itself. Only now do we realize what this means to us in person. However right away I feel constrained to take this 'us' back because more accurately, and with a colder eye to our popular affability, do I express it in the following way: I recognize what it means to me in person and you recognize what it means to you in person.

After all, the Jesus-experience is not an experience for man in general. Society knows nothing of it. To each it occurs "in his own language", this is what I mean to say.

Neither, however, is it an individualistic experience. Whoever desires to realize the god-idea entirely on his own and out of his own individuality will be overcome by it and of this experience I can personally tell a tale or two.

Actually it is the case that every human being who wishes to realize the godly essence that occurs to him errs invariably to some extent on the side of the massive or on that of the individualistic, however this may be rectified afterwards. The godly never completely fits into our being, however well we are prepared. It has to overflow. Not what overflows but what is in the container – in the proverbial cup – is ours.

So the live Jesus-experience is neither massive nor individualistic but – communal. Where two or three are joined – in preparation for Jesus – there Jesus presents himself.

Oh, he who is angry, with those few who experience Jesus today, for their unavoidable minimum of error, his heart is surely stone, and here the word of the historic Jesus is apt, when he corrects those who would criticize the celebrating crowd as he rides into Jerusalem: "If these did not rejoice, surely the stones would."

*

Now let us make the following more tangible: the realization of the godly when it impresses us as idea or notion; the shaping of the mighty, violent or forceful notion once we personally consent to the experience; the contemporary embodiment and spiritualization of the notion we have of the godly – as embodiment – .

*

Just now it occurs to me – I have the notion – that I can do you some good if I not only wish you well but at the same time I also believe that this actually does you good. Right away I am overcome by a sort of melancholy, because I not only recognize the truth of this idea but I also sense the responsibility that accompanies it. If it's true that I can do you good whether you know of it or not, then surely I should do this now, right away, for I can see how you are beset by sorrows and how you bury yourself truculently in your indifference to me. Surely it doesn't matter who bears the blame for it. Blame and atonement, guilt and punishment, who would waste the time with that, who would spoil his day with it. Could we not love one another quite regardless of whether we like one another? At the moment you don't like me, you even very much dislike me, and that, so far as I can see, makes your life a misery. You feel I am your enemy and instead of loving me, in order to rid yourself of this animosity, you do this and that instead and you don't love your enemy. However I cannot make you do it because you freely have to arrive at this decision yourself. What I can do myself, that is what matters to me; and I have to say that it's not all the same to me whether you love or hate me. It makes a difference to me, and this difference I call fear and I experience it as trembling. Not merely because you hate me but because it's you who hate me, that is what undermines my soul. I am resolved to bear this and to re-establish my equilibrium again and again – and as a matter of fact for you sake. In this way I also do it for the sake of Jesus, in that I do it for our sake. Or is that not so? Why, in any case, do I talk here of Jesus? Surely it should suffice that I do this for your sake. What does Jesus have to do with it?

Well, possibly that will come to me. In the meanwhile we are advised not to be afraid. And right away I am reminded of a word uttered by the historic Jesus: "Fear not, for I am always with you, even to the end." So there, in that sense, fear has long ago been conquered, as a destructive force, and there is really and truly no reason for me to be afraid of fear. Out of this quaking and trembling I make a limitless terror for myself because I am afraid of fear and do not bravely look it in the eye and know it as a conquered force. Not I, but it, is the conquered might and for that I have the guarantee of my knowledge regarding the messianic success.

That I love you, in spite of your hate, this you surely can see when I describe like this how I behave in relation to you. Here I write it down on paper, but if I had no paper I would surely prove it to you by way of my behaviour and my expressed sensibility.

I even regret right now that I mentioned the name Jesus above, I don't quite know why. What was I trying to achieve? Maybe I wanted to influence you by way of some magical touch? I am not at all clear about that.

And what I have quite forgotten, with all my demonstrations and arguments, is the principal part of my idea, namely that when I wish to do you good, it helps that I know you are actually helped. This knowing, which at the same time is a believing, I will keep awake in myself for a while now. It seems to be a rather special knowing, as I know I influence you to the good even if I am not in the same room with you at the moment. It should be enough to say: I should know that it happens and that it works. However it seems to be necessary to express this as follows: I must know that it takes place – so that it will take place. What a strange duplication! Ah well, the main thing is, I understand and know what I do and mean. If you now accuse me and throw curses at my head, then those are externalities, that in no way contradict the success of my doing. After all it's not my business to imagine a success of my good doing but to love you and to stand in for you, in the knowledge that this does you good whether you know it or not. Of course I would much prefer that you loved me rather than hating me, and I can tell you something about that right now. Whoever hates is not free, and the love in the presence of an enemy surely rests on a certain freedom. Therefore I have no intention to persuade you to love me, nor to like me either, but I carry the wish to rid us of this hatred of yours by way of love, so that you too are free of it. How long this will take I cannot possibly know.

Fear wears down the valour of my soul. I have to say, I am ashamed that under certain conditions I invariably am afraid. Confronted by a hysterical female I turn into a coward, and that has to change. That I become quite brutal then, even if only inwardly, that goes without saying. Fear robs us of our confidence, so that we no longer think and feel, nor do we act or suffer, and human affection is right away done for. I don't like to think of all the nonsense I have committed, being false, dishonest or unclean! In the presence of everyone I say this: There where in my case always fear arises, there position yourself, live Jesus of whom I know. Even more than believing in god, I know you. So please be present where my fear arises and be the unending courage of my soul. For this I ask and pray. What use are all my faculties, if at a critical moment fear again tears the soul out of my heart and I become unreal? Once I am unreal, what use to me is the true and beautiful?

Apparently there are some who can love on the spur of the moment when hatred screams. For this I wish.

*

61

In the end we rely on live experiences of notions and ideas themselves, for we have to do here with Jesus in our heart, where otherwise the will had its way, with all its egoistic ideals and its egotistic sorties.

The notion we experience signifies in three ways: <u>Firstly</u> we intercept it in our soul, as humour or mood. Good or bad humour or mood signify in the same way that something godly has entered us, forcefully; and it points to or indicates the notion itself. The 'that' and the 'where' of the notion becomes present to us. Now we rely on our temperament, because we don't want to become moody, acquire a bad mood or humour, or suchlike. Mood and humour themselves are nothing but signs, that is a very difficult lesson, because most of the time we suppose that when we are in a good mood and good humoured that this is a sign of life itself, that it should please and satisfy us and on the basis of such a misunderstanding a mania develops, if Jesus is in our heart. Temperament implies restraint and endurance. Similarly, in the case of bad mood or humour, it appears that often, if we are not careful, we fear a threat or some danger, which is just as wrong and develops into depression.

What we refer to as manic-depressive therefore originates in false evaluation, or follows in the train of an avoided or wasted evaluation – of mood and humour. The correct evaluation sees both of these, equally whether good or bad, pleasant or unpleasant, as quite simply what is the case and what allows us to infer a notion or idea, so that we really do well not to concentrate at all on our mood or humour, good or bad, nor on the state of our soul at all but rather on the idea or notion, or better, on the godly being that is now live in us.

An idea implies that a godly being is live in us and a mood or a humour implies that something is the case, (es ist der Fall) and that the time has come for it (dass es fällig ist). Temperament, again, is the faculty by means of which we bear this circumstance (das Fällige) for a time; that we appreciate it attentively and deal with it honourably.

We bear it. Temperament is a case of bearing the soul that is affected by mood or humour, or both.

If we know nothing of the godly and if we do not understand how mood and humour point to this godly being that is now live in us, we may well entertain enthusiasm and high spirits until we become quite unreasonable – or else we suppose that the whole world (which does not exist) rests on our shoulders. Genius becomes melancholy or demonic and often both at once. The artist turns into a diagnostician of Society and to a symptom of Society. He become critical and finds himself in a critical situation. All this on account of his misunderstanding of the real situation. Temperament in that case cannot develop. Experiences appear to be unbearable. Instead of temperament, a craving develops for alcohol, for abusive drugs – for suicide. Mood swings disseminate unrest, cause uncertainty.

So this is of primary importance, that the idea or notion is correctly perceived. That we know of the forceful ways and means of ideas and notions and prepare thoroughly for them, so that: "when the flood comes, the house stands on stone and not on sand". It is important that we do not delude ourselves about humour and mood, preferring the so-called good over the bad. Whether pleasant or unpleasant, melancholy or high spirited, this must not impress us as important or even interesting, because we have learnt – and have been brought up and educated – to infer right away the live godly being, so that we may attain to it. Meanwhile we bear it in good and even temper. Equanimity needs to be practiced and exercised. Just as we need to guard against defiance, against rage and fury, we must also take precautions against melancholy, depression and unstable indifference.

Before we arrive at the second point, let's direct our attention to the fact that the godly is live in us and not massive, not material. Live here implies eternally living, immortal – which explains suicide. He who is unprepared and has no understanding must clear the way for that which lives eternally in itself. That which is live already is, has being, true or real, and suddenly, forcefully if not violently, it turns up within us, so no wonder that so much depends on the comparison between it and us. And no wonder that Jesus prepared his disciples when he sent them out into he cities and among the people, and that he quite rightly predicted for them the event (notion, idea) of the son of man, however not yet his coming on the clouds of heaven as strength. The godly as idea was dramatically foretold here – "even before you have finished with the cities of Israel". We should take note of this before we suppose Jesus was mistaken. The kingdom was not yet here, but near.

*

In the <u>second</u> place, then, let us just examine the role imagination and fantasy play here - and can play, if we behave wisely. What we want to keep in mind is that imagination and fantasy are hale and hearty only if they are active within wisdom, when they act wisely. And of course what we mean here is not the wisdom of the learned but that of children, the childlike or little wisdom crucial for bringing that which lives eternal to our recognition. And once we have this wisdom, which is neither obstinate nor poisonous, then we right away also possess imagination and fantasy, that appear again only in separation wisely. Wisdom as the mother gives birth to them as her children. What is all too often and commonly called imagination and fantasy either does not know this mother or is wrenched out of her prematurely. Then, too, one attempts insanely to provoke them by way of excitation, artificially and artistically, and that is a pity.

*

Why, in any case, do we speak of fantasy and imagination separately instead of simply saying wisdom? The live-godly being that enters us, that occurs to us (das uns einfällt), the idea, in other words, that impresses itself upon us, always has such an effect of separating. We recognize the "sword" that Jesus brought. 'Things' are separated and then newly joined. It is crucial for us to be aware of this mystery, for the sake of our spiritual health, because this separation is visited upon us without our contribution or agreement, forcefully, "when we least know", but the "making one of the two", as Thomas the apostle wrote, is up to us and depends on us. To welcome Jesus, then, means both, holding ourselves in readiness for the separation of our being and at least participating in the making-one, at the beginning, in the middle and at the end. All that is to come, as future, in the realm of notion and idea (no need to mention angels and laws every time), becomes understandable in view of this. And I repeat here, that in this essay we concern ourselves with Jesus, and with Jesus today, in our hearts, not foremost with Jesus the Messiah in the god-realm. Whoever elects to stand in solidarity with the Messiah, as friend, or at least subordinates himself to him, as belonging to the realm and as companion in the work, he also has Jesus in his heart and knows of him there, as historical and dear. However not everyone whose heart inclines to Jesus, ideally or lawfully, which is to say principally, and who knows of the true and the beautiful, also has, at the same time, the messianic being in his own being. Jesus is the Messiah, that is certain, however not everyone who knows him as Jesus understands him as Messiah. Yet no one can understand Him as Messiah who does not readily have him in his heart – truly, beautifully and historically. Understanding Jesus as Messiah is matter for the few, who can then make it available for a few, several or many. However the knowing about Jesus, about the affectionate Jesus in our hearts on whom, ultimately, all our human affection for one another depends, (after we have, separate from one another, left all our old, popular affection and sociability behind) – this knowing is, on one side, an ultimate security, satisfaction and rest, but on the other side it forever urges and drives, truly and beautifully, towards messianic understanding and messianic perception.

In the same way as we not only say knowledge but separately understanding and perception, so we also say not only wisdom, but separately imagination and fantasy. Both are separate only so that they 'might be' joined. Our rank as honourable human beings depends upon this.

*

The idea we perceive (conceive) and temperamentally support (bear) should now also be wisely handled (dealt with). Insofar as we say 'should' and to the extent that there is still an urgency, wisdom separates into imagination and fantasy. In order to handle something we need both hands, imagination on the right and fantasy on the left.

What all we now imagine, under the remaining pressure of the forceful idea, this must not be believed right away. What we have imagined does not become strong until we pull ourselves together and create room, and place, for fantasy, because, reluctant as we may be to accept this, our fantasy is the bridge to reality. If we cannot manage properly with our faculty for fantasy, we can never be quite secure in the believing we do. Due to prejudice we repress something human in ourselves that we cannot otherwise attain to. What it is we repress, mostly denying it on rational grounds, cannot be given another name.

So it is precisely with our fantasy that we find ourselves on the border where the knowing of Jesus in our heart transcends to the perceptive understanding of Messianic being. Imagination is not a power until we draw the Messianic dignity of Jesus into the realm of our experience – as live experience. Fantasy can therefore also be seen as the link for the purpose of connecting mere experience with live experience.

In this way then the live godly being becomes – live experience. As a result we stand firmly connected with the godly and only now do we become genuinely human too.

There is no such thing as imagination without fantasy. That would then be mere imagination, in other words a miserable decomposition, due to which fantasy too gets a bad name, because popularly fantasy is nothing but mere, disembodied imagination with a fantastic colouring. Concentration is required, if we hope to cut through this prejudicial chaos. Many get stuck and are then plagued, because they try to serve two masters, one popular, who insists exclusively on Society and money, prestige and reputation, and the other, who is individualistic and addicted to sensual happiness, to the pride and honour of his personality. Both are idolatry.

If we approach what is live and godly with imagination rich in fantasy, cognizant of our soul and not without temperament, this turns us into honourable human beings, for whom Jesus is not merely some historical image or fantastic figment but personal life. The idea we perceive (in our soul) and endure (temperamentally) we then experience, live, (with fantasy), and in this way our life becomes complete. So we have progressed up to this point, in our examination, where now Messianic being lovingly streams into us – and where we then at the same time too influence our human environment.

*

Dealing wisely with the contemporary idea, with what has occurred to us presently in our soul as mood or humour, we have further work now and we intend to take our time. Above we spoke of "the shaping of the mighty, violent or forceful notion once we personally consent to the experience of it". With wisdom, as imagination and fantasy, we get ahead, and this 'getting ahead', so that we do not get stuck, moody-depressive or manic-overwrought, is crucial and we will give it a little more thought.

Our consent to the idea should be personal, so it seems right to us. Nonetheless the effect of every idea on us is individualistic. Not individual but individualistic. This is due to the forceful or violent being of the idea. We react automatically individualistic, rigidly, arrogantly and defiantly, or conceited, vain and self-seeking, to every idea that occurs to us forcefully. The difference between, on one hand, individuality, our ability to stand alone in the hope of becoming personal and on the other hand individualism, our being self-obsessed in contradiction to the personal, should be emphasized here. Individualism implies that we get stuck with our mood or humour, good or bad and that therefore we cannot or do not want to descend from a 'high' and that we cannot or do not wish to rise from a 'low'. Arrogance and mockery alternate with dejection and vanity. As soon as individualism strives systematically towards some goal, catastrophe is not long to follow.

Nevertheless the initial reaction to every forceful idea is invariably individualistic. The son of man must come when we're not looking, so be attentive. How much wisdom is given us in this word of Jesus! The coming of the son of man can then be a continually repeated experience, in other words a live experience now of the future son of man, surely that is a tremendous joy for us! That our future is so utterly replete with the live and godly and that it shines, refulgent as godly being, surely that is the result of this wise insight – and an eternally human outlook.

*

Now there is only one way out of this unavoidable initial individualism, and that is contempt of oneself. However pure self-contempt is destructive, pessimistic, cynical and so on, and it brings us nothing because it does not let us get on. It must be a self-contempt in the name and for the sake of that which is brought home to us as idea, as notion, and why not as Messianic being right away. If we are able to surmise from our soul-disposition that something eternal and live must have entered into us, then we, as intelligent human beings, should not find it too hard now right away to make that inward movement, so that right away we can push ourselves away from our individualistic self in order to prepare and make space for the eternally human. The first time is of course always the most difficult, because then this is a case of the idea or notion as such, since Jesus has not yet moved into our Heart. Thereafter however it gets simpler and the critical act becomes habitual.

As soon as we have come up with contempt for our self, sufficiently, for the sake of what has been borne into us, the idea actually takes shape – is no longer idea but shape (Gestalt). The godly/human shapes or embodies itself for us and – we participate.

This participation is then our doing. We act, inasmuch as we simply witness what goes on – and what is being done specifically for our sake. It happens for us and it is done for us and if we would like to have the benefit of it we bear witness – for others.

Here now we stand with total equanimity before our ethical requirement, and before the explanation of why, here, after we disproved our individualism some time ago and have even discarded our individuality as such, we must come out and away from Society as such and from every closed community and self-defined commune, in order to enter upon the great rejoicing of our personal reality.

Individuality as such, even though it does not unify and contradict what is personally real, like individualism, nonetheless we cannot take it, as such, with us into our personal being because as individuals we can know and recognize only other individuals and not persons. As an individual I cannot communicate myself, while communication is the being, or at least the one side of the being, of personality. Two individuals, so to speak, always talk past each other. They suppose they agree but they are deaf and blind for one another's pain and wellbeing. They delude themselves and in reality they do not participate and they do not communicate. What happens then is that Society consists of individuals and whoever

studies Society is bound to come to the conclusion that he is dealing with cells in an organism, with links in a chain, where each
individual motivates himself and is motivated by the group, as if
nothing else existed. And a closed community again is an individual, an individuality once over, or an Ersatz-Individualism,
whereas surely we might stand in for one another, not like an exclusive community, whose God belongs to that community and
not to every member. Because every community that stands out
and dissociates itself from others is again, on account of this, unreal and contrary to the god-realm.

What we do in love for one another must therefore be done in
the spirit of merciful love, which is god and that is the purpose and
goal of every idea and notion, so that we will neither hide the eternally human being that is now within us nor fear the returning son
of man, but we will participate and cooperate in his growth (Gestalt) while we communicate and share ourselves out.

*

The transformation of the individual into the personal is then
the third issue we intend to examine, in reference to the ideal notion and notions as such.

We know after all how poorly we customarily manage with our
identification of ourselves as body and mind, as flesh and spirit, and
how everything we touch disintegrates into spiritual and carnal
pieces, because we suppose that the one is grand and the other secure. God, however, will not be tied down and we cannot think
highly of man. As a consequence people get lost in their own misery
and the god to whom they belong must get on without them.

With that in mind, we can say that every idea that occurs to us
heals, or previous to that it is holy, because it presses into us at
once humanly and godly, bodily and mentally, and that we must
believe. Our peculiar human natural believing is perfectly suitable
for this because it bears within itself the predisposition for what

can be simultaneously thought and sensed. Once again, happy is he who believes without having to see.

However if we don't know how to believe and if this primary human faculty is overlaid or paralyzed, then, what would occur to us if we were capable of believing, affects us nevertheless and so we are beset by obstinacy. Obstinately we try, somehow, to ignore the absence in ourselves of the ability to believe. So it cannot happen otherwise than that the physical and spiritual element of that which has been introduced into us must occur to us as contradictory and antithetical, and this we will then feel obliged to explain. The entire modern age, in all fields and in all regions, is interspersed with such attempts at explanation, which in themselves are symptomatic of people's inability, basically and fundamentally, to believe. One could well say that the blame lies with the manufacture of dogma, except what else are dogmas if not signs of the fact that believing has become petrified and spoiled as beliefs.

In order to enjoy Jesus personally in our hearts today we must be able to believe, - while each and every belief as such fundamentally prevents us from doing so, and once again, he who has no belief may be closer to the goal of true and beautiful reality than the one who has one. If he stands no closer, then at least he does not stand quite so far away.

How can we learn to believe again? If someone admits as much and says: Yes indeed, sadly that seems to be the case, I have lost the ability to believe, for the bodily and the mental do indeed seem to contradict each other and seem to be antithetical for me, and even though I had a belief, with which I could grandiosely and in the most complicated manner override and ignore this bothersome contradiction, I have nonetheless now lost it again: well, his belief could not have amounted to much, because once we really and truly possess something we can never lose it. So now I am back where I was, when I still had no belief and – possibly still believed.

*

71

Surely that is not such a stupid theory, that a belief will drive away our ability to believe. To children who want bread, we give stones. They might well be precious stones but are no more digestible or nourishing for that. Whoever harnesses a child's brain into a formal creed, of whatever persuasion, what does he do for that child's human natural capacity to believe? Surely it is beside the point now whether he turns into a heathen or a Christian, this little man, if he ceases to be a human being!

Let us concentrate on the new teaching that Jesus transfers into our hearts, that here, where we have become less than human, we may become human again. Because the greatest possible dignity, even since our birth, is to be human. How can I become the human being I always have been – only I didn't know it, because I was cut off from my origin by means of ignorance and nonsense?

As soon as a contradiction opens for me between body and mind, between matter and light, between love and understanding, the time has come for me to believe. Such a contradiction is a sign that there is more to believe. Incidentally it is also a sign that I did not sufficiently believe, although mainly it is a sign that there is more to believe. So mainly it is a good and happy sign – and only coincidentally an unhappy and bad one. That which is incidental only exists to remind us of the main matter, so that we do it and are guided by it.

But now most people suppose it is impossible to believe except that one believes – in something, something we can picture or imagine, and in something that has a name and an identification. Surely a belief must have some content. Yes, surely, this is true of a belief, of any belief, this one or that one, perhaps a Christian or a heathen one. After all, a belief is a form and a form has content, this is as correct as that one and one make two, and even if someone proudly insists "my belief is the belief", then this is all the more a form with content, or arrogantly and bull-headed the form with that content, and "there is no such thing as blinkers!"

A belief, any belief, must have content and has it too, little or much, grand and marvellous or worthless to the point of blatant nonsense – but believing, human and god-original believing, that has no content, because it isn't a form, and it has no contents because it isn't a formality. Just as a tree, after all, is not a hole, because a hole consists, does it not, of a nothing in something, and whoever comes along and would show me a nothing in the absence of something, well, I have to doubt his good sense. Now if he even suggests I should leap into that nothing without something, and he would persuade me I cannot be happy until I have performed such a salto mortale into it, well, then I can only turn away. That is when Jesus went up into the hills of Caesarea Philippi.

No, this original human faculty of believing has neither content nor form, nor is it content or form, because this conceptual analysis of form/content is itself a symptom of the contradictory and the antithetical, which lets us know: there is more to believe.

Now if someone comes along and tells us, in view of these opposites, the following: "neither the one nor the other", like for example the Buddha, is that then a belief, or is it the original and real believing? Neither. Neither a belief nor believing but a presentiment it is of real believing, and this presentiment relieves us of tension and strife and of obstinacy, however in no way does it acquaint anyone with original human believing, which rests entirely within itself, for which reason it promotes that organic growth of godly human beings (or of human gods).

Whoever really believes, he grows organically as a human being, (not as a rational animal, nor as a heathen, nor as a Christian) and there is no reason for him to wait until he gets caught up in one of those contradictions or antitheses. However if he does get caught up, then especially he believes, because then, after all, he has proof: firstly, that at the moment he does not believe, (not any longer or not yet), and secondly, that here is something more to believe.

Only then is there <u>something</u> to believe, if we are caught up in a contradiction or are confronted by an antithesis, otherwise we believe simply and to the point.

Simple believing connects us with what is old and precise believing connects with what is new. But that is one and the same believing, here more turned towards the old or there more directed towards the new. For all that pertains to us as members of the god-realm in reality is old and desires to be new or else is new and wishes to care and stand in for what is old. Human growth corresponds to the godly effect and purpose of our father and all our original believing is really more like a childlike confidence in this contemporary paternal effectiveness, which naturally includes Jesus in our hearts, as a recipe for existence and survival. He who only exists, does not yet live, no matter what he believes, and whoever merely survives, he no longer lives, no matter what sort of a belief he follows or what kind of creed he witnesses.

When we say we believe in god, then we either say nothing more than that we believe, or we have to add that this is no contradictory or antithetical god. God is spirit, while good spirit, or whatever is good-spiritual, does not contradict the bodily; but the bad-spiritual does contradict the bodily. Neither is there a contradiction between the good-spiritual and the bad-spiritual – that we don't delude ourselves about this or get lost in it – but the bad-spiritual contradicts the good-spiritual and opposes it, while the good-spiritual does not oppose and contradict the bad-spiritual, as if there were possible some arrangement by argument on a common basis. It simply asserts itself as the good-spiritual and the bad disappears again. Let us put it like this, like a child: our god knows that the bad is powerless and without being, in comparison to him. Thence our simple and precise confidence, and our unconditional trust.

If now, while we think and feel, such a typical contradiction between mind and body, or between spirit and flesh, comes to our attention within us, then we do well right away to believe, especially inasmuch as we know how our faculty of belief becomes

74

stronger while we ourselves, as human and more personal beings, hold ourselves, live and with a living heart, into this contradiction and opposition. In other words, we endure. It is a sensible enduring, for we know what we are doing and why we do it: we believe, because there is something to believe and because of the opportunity for growth in our personal humanity.

We can always believe and we do well always to believe but if we endure temperately in our live believing when we find ourselves in some contradiction or stand confronted by some opposition, then our believing too becomes stronger, becomes more flexible, more pliant, finer and more versatile.

Most of the time, when we come up against some contradiction, we don't become aware of it and right away we are implicated in it and fabricate arguments in order to annihilate or to settle it and often we succeed in this too – to a degree and for a time. Believing is not a synthesis and does not bring about a synthesis, nor does it resolve (aufheben) a contradiction. A dialectic does not know of itself. But the original, human-creaturely believing is wise, so that we become aware of any contradiction, right away and then, and so that we know: at this very moment I am holding out, enduring, in the presence of this contradiction. I don't endure stupidly before it, like an animal, nor livelessly, like some sacrificial victim. For which reason the historical Jesus, strictly speaking, was no sacrifice, for the sacrifice is stupid and dumb, while Jesus, right up to the last, acted and was demonstrably live, mainly even in that he demonstrated for us what it means really to believe, as he grew, meanwhile, into his messianic dignity. Applying the concept of the sacrificial victim to this trusting activity is excessively metaphoric, understandable enough under certain circumstances but nonetheless overstrained.

*

"I have no belief", someone says, "neither can I believe." – and that in itself is an antithesis, of which one might be able to help him become aware. After all he believes what he says, else he would not say it. What he says, what he expresses, that he believes. No one, therefore, can say: "I cannot believe". At most this would be an aberration of the mind. The worst we can say of ourselves confirms, in spite of everything else, that we believe, except perhaps unconsciously. Because we do not know what is required for believing, and because we mostly think and sense in contradictions and antitheses, the believing that we do does not come to our attention and so we do not have the true benefit of it.

Jesus in my heart knows how fundamental it is for my being here that I believe and so he supplies me daily with occasions for discovering this faculty: by confronting me either in body or in mind with problems that can only be solved by believing. Imagine, these problems are not bodily <u>and</u> mental but bodily <u>or</u> mental. A bodily problem, for example is typically a mountain over which I cannot get. A thing prevents me from getting where I want to get. Whether or not I can imagine that thing accurately, that makes no difference, only it seems that something has to be dreamed away before I can achieve my goal. I cannot continue to write, because I haven't a notion what to write. Why not? Because I am too stupid, too dull. This dullness is a thing between me and my intention, and so it constitutes a bodily problem, without all mental complication. If I now tackle this dullness, simply and precisely, just so as it always seems and without any attempts at complicated interpretation or explanation, I sense, perhaps, within me, something like a stubbornness, and I can add that on right away to the bodily thing that will not get out of my way. Then there appears, perhaps, a feeling of hatred, of anxiety, of impatience or even of despair, and all this I may observe as further examples of the bodily obstruction that prevents me problematically from realizing my wishes. Everything possible rises up and adds itself on to my problem. Perhaps there is a reason why this problem presents itself to me. This I must know and I must remain reminded of it. The problem exists for me because I still do not believe or believe enough.

What means 'believe enough'? The solution of the problem. The mountain throws itself into the sea as soon as I am rightly and thoroughly oriented in terms of my believing and no one can tell me how long this should take. I should know however that this pure believing brings me steadily closer to the solution – even though I cannot sense that.

Believing leaves no tracks. In this it is different from meaning, which leaves something sensible. For example, we cannot exert ourselves to believe and there is no such thing as methodical or technical believing. I occupy myself here so extensively with this matter because I know that Jesus in our heart does not rest until we have learned to believe and have once again made a habit of it. Until then, he promptly sends us problems, bodily and mental, and instead of complaining we should really be grateful. Your car stops in the middle of the traffic. A bodily problem of an outward kind. You may know right away what the issue is here. Your main wish should not be this outward matter, that the car without fail must once again be running, but that your believing functions and gets stronger and that you as a human being become more human, more genuine and complete. Just by the way you may concern yourself with the car and the traffic too.

To believe means to be human and to become human and to believe means right away to believe in god, this we always have to add; actually we cannot even do otherwise, so original as our father is this believing. Whoever believes, makes use of the inherited affinity to his heavenly father.

Inwardly and outwardly we come across bodily problems, to which at first we do not seem to be able to measure up, until we recall that every problem exists for the sake of our believing and our growth.

So not only the bodily but also the mental and spiritual problems would return us to this confidence and to this trust. Madness, insanity, any derangement of the mind, those are mental or spiritual problems, as we call them, because this time the body is not without spirit but the spirit appears to be without body. There is no doubt that this is appearance and not reality. However in order to recognize it as appearance, we need the fundamental human faculty of believing. While we do not believe, we cannot but confuse this appearance with reality.

In reality, mind and body cannot be separate, for this the existence of the Messiah is our guarantee and all that we understand under god-realm, or reality. Bodiless spirit or mind, then, is an illusion just as mindless or spiritless body is an error. However if now we see the fuss and fluster we human beings often kick up when the fire of the Messiah presses into us in order to make us 'believable', then it seems as if our human intelligence must surely be in doubt. How often do we not behave as if we had to fight our way through or as if we needed to be punished or as if there were no way out from the many unbelievable dangers in which we stray, only because our good god steps closer to us! We can imagine the difficulties of our merciful father. If he stays away from us, we go to pieces and as soon as he approaches us, we scream and behave as though we were crazy. Mercy itself stands confronted here by a problem, which is called: a human being unwilling to believe. Such a human being is impossible for love. Therefore we should take care of one another, because otherwise so much humanity perishes, on account of a lack of believing.

There is no need for us to fight our way through, we do not need to be punished and there is a way out of the innumerable dangers that exaggerate our anxiety and our fear so much. This way out is believing, which we can learn and practise in terms of these spiritual and carnal, bodily and mental problems, since for that purpose we are endowed with them. Perhaps we first have to struggle through to an understanding of our humanity as in danger, however the problems are not the danger and no part of the danger but they are divine initiative and deliverance. We are to be rescued out of an actual danger of which we often are in no way aware.

The ongoing loss of humanity does not hurt. Often one even feels rather good at the time. Most often however we cannot feel it at all. Our total degeneration goes on quietly and in the dark. A remnant however – the famous remnant: if we will not rescue ourselves and if we do not rescue that remnant, then it must at last be done even contrary to our will, and that may well be the saddest of god's works, when a father finally has to bow out of the relationship with his son because his son just plain no longer knows him. He does not believe. Not that he defiantly refuses to believe, but he just plain does not believe.

So one deludes oneself and speaks of heaven and hell, as if the decision eventually fell out in that direction. However the ultimate resolve is called being or non-being, is called life or nothing. Not that we must still be saved but that god must save himself from us and with eternal sorrow he must distance himself from us and withdraw into himself. This withdrawal of god from us is not painful for us. What is painful and embarrassing, terrible and shameful for us, are the attempts at rescue by god, as he stands in for us – as Jesus in our heart – today.

* * *

www.ingramcontent.com/pod-product-compliance
Lightning Source LLC
Chambersburg PA
CBHW060110300526
45791CB00018B/999